The  PHRASEBOOK
FRENCH

English edition prepared by First Edition Translations Ltd,
Great Britain
Designed and produced by AA Publishing
First published in 1995 as Wat & Hoe Frans,
© Kosmos Uitgevers B.V. – Utrecht/Antwerpen

This edition © AA Media Limited 2008
Reprinted July 2008, October 2009, January and April 2010 and
April 2011

ISBNs: 978-0-7495-5664-8 (SS) and 25170931 (Aldi)

A CIP catalogue record for this book is available from the
British Library

Published by AA Publishing (a trading name of AA Media Limited)
whose registered office is Fanum House, Basingstoke, Hampshire
RG21 4EA. Registered number 06112600.

Printed and bound in Italy by Printer Trento S.r.l.

Find out more about AA Publishing and the wide range of
services the AA provides by visiting our website at theAA.com/shop

A04690

Contents

Introduction

● **Welcome to the AA's Pocket Guide Phrase Books series,**
covering the most popular European languages and containing
everything you'd expect from a comprehensive language series.
They're concise, accessible and easy to understand, and you'll find
them indispensable on your trip abroad.

Each guide is divided into 14 themed sections and starts with a
pronunciation table which gives you the phonetic spelling to all the
words and phrases you'll need to know for your trip.

Throughout the book you'll come across coloured boxes with a 🗨
beside them. These are designed to help you if you can't understand
what your listener is saying to you. Hand the book over to them and
encourage them to point to the appropriate answer to the question
you are asking.

Other coloured boxes in the book – this time without the symbol –
give alphabetical listings of themed words with their English
translations beside them.

This phrase book covers all subjects you are likely to come across
during the course of your visit, from reserving a room for the night
to ordering food and drink at a restaurant and what to do if your car
breaks down or you lose your traveller's cheques and money. With
over 2,000 commonly used words and essential phrases at your
fingertips you can rest assured that you will be able to get by in
all situations.

Pronunciation table

The pronunciation provided should be read as if it were English, bearing in mind the following main points:

Vowels

a, à or â	a in man	ah	table	tahbl
é	like a in make	ay	été	aytay
è, ê, e	like ai in air	eh	rêve	rehv
e	sometimes like u in fluff	uh	le, ne, je, me	luh, nuh, jhuh, muh
i	like ee in seen	ee	si	see
ô	like o in foam	oa	hôtel	oatehl
o	like o in John	o	homme	om
	sometimes like ô	oa	arroser	ahroasay
u	between ee and ew	ew	tu	tew

Combinations of letters which represent vowel sounds:

ez, er	similar to é	ay	louer	looay
ais, ait	the eh sound	eh	fait	feh
au, eau	similar to ô	oa	beau	boa
ail	like i in side	ahy	travail	trahvahy
ei	similar to è	eh	Seine	sehn
eille	eh + y as in yes	ehy	bouteille	bootehy
eu	similar to e above	uh	feu	fuh
iè	ye as in yes	yeh	siècle	syehkl
ié, ier, iez	y + the ay sound	yay	janvier	jhohnvyay
ille	ee + y as in yes	eey	famille	fameey
oi, oy	combines w + a	wah	moi	mwah
ou, oû	oo as in hoot	oo	vous	voo
ui	combines w and ee	wee	cuir	kweer

Consonants

ch	like **sh** in **sh**ine	sh	**chaud**	shoa
ç	like **s** in **s**ome	s	**garçon**	gahrsawn
g	before **e**, **i** and **y**			
	like **s** in lei**s**ure	jh	**nager**	nahjhay
	before **a**, **o** and **u**			
	like **g** in **g**ot	g	**gâteau**	gahtoa
gn	like **ny** in can**y**on	ny	**agneau**	ahnyoa
h	silent			
j	like **s** in lei**s**ure	jh	**jour**	jhoor
qu	like **k** in **k**ind	k	**que**	kuh
r	rolled at the back of the throat			
w	like **v** in **v**ine	v	**wagonlit**	vahgawnlee

Nasal sounds

Nasal sounds are written in French by adding an n to a vowel or a combination of vowels pronounced as the English ng:

an/am, **en/em**	a little like **song**	ohn	**français,** **lentement**	frohnseh, lohntmohn
in/im, ain, **aim, ein**	a little like **bang**	ahn	**instant, faim**	ahnstohn, fahn
on/om	a nasal form of **awn**	awn	**non**	nawn
un/um	a little like **rung**	uhn	**un**	uhn
ien	**y** + the **ahn** sound	yahn	**bien**	byahn

1 Useful lists

1.1 Today or tomorrow?

What day is it today? __ C'est quel jour aujourd'hui?
seh kehl jhoor oajhoordwee?

Today's Monday _____ Aujourd'hui c'est lundi
oajhoordwee seh luhndee

– Tuesday _____ Aujourd'hui c'est mardi
oajhoordwee seh mahrdee

– Wednesday _____ Aujourd'hui c'est mercredi
oajhoordwee seh mehrkruhdee

– Thursday_____ Aujourd'hui c'est jeudi
oajhoordwee seh jhuhdee

– Friday _____ Aujourd'hui c'est vendredi
oajhoordwee seh vohndruhdee

– Saturday _____ Aujourd'hui c'est samedi
oajhoordwee seh sahmdee

– Sunday _____ Aujourd'hui c'est dimanche
oajhoordwee seh deemohnsh

in January _____ en janvier
ohn jhohnvyay

since February _____ depuis février
duhpwee fayvryay

in spring_____ au printemps
oa prahntohn

in summer _____ en été; l'été
ohn naytay; laytay

in autumn_____ en automne
ohn noatonn

in winter _____ en hiver; l'hiver
ohn neevehr; leevehr

1998 _____ mille neuf cent quatre-vingt-dix-huit
meel nuhf sohn kahtr vahn dee zweet

the twentieth century___ le vingtième siècle
luh vahntyehm syehkl

What's the date today?_ Quelle est la date aujourd'hui?
kehl eh lah daht oajhoordwee?

Today's the 24th_____	Aujourd'hui on est le vingt-quatre *oajhoordwee awn neh luh vahnkahtr*
Monday 3 November___ 1997	lundi, le trois novembre 1997 *luhndee, luh trwah novohnbr meel nuhf* *sohn kahtr vahn dee seht*
in the morning_____	le matin *luh mahtahn*
in the afternoon _____	l'après-midi *lahpreh meedee*
in the evening _____	le soir *luh swahr*
at night_____	la nuit *lah nwee*
this morning _____	ce matin *suh mahtahn*
this afternoon _____	cet après-midi *seht ahpreh meedee*
this evening_____	ce soir *suh swahr*
tonight _____	ce soir *suh swahr*
last night _____	hier soir *yehr swahr*
this week_____	cette semaine *seht suhmehn*
next month _____	le mois prochain *luh mwah proshahn*
last year_____	l'année passée *lahnay pahsay*
next..._____	prochain/prochaine *proshahn/proshehn*
in...days/weeks/ _____ months/years	dans...jours/semaines/mois/ans *dohn...jhoor/suhmehn/mwah/ohn*
...weeks ago _____	il y a...semaines *eel ee ah...suhmehn*
day off _____	jour de congé *jhoor duh kawnjhay*

1.2 Bank holidays

● **The most important** Bank holidays in France are the following:

January 1	Le Jour de l'An (New Year's Day)
March/April	Pâques, (Easter)
	le lundi de Pâques (Easter Monday)
May 1	La Fête du Travail (May Day; Labour Day)
May 8	Le Jour de la Libération (Liberation Day)
May/June	L'Ascension; la Pentecôte (Ascension; Whit Sunday)
July 14	La Fête Nationale (Bastille Day)
August 15	L'Assomption (Assumption)
November 1	La Toussaint (All Saints' Day)
November 11	L'Armistice (Armistice Day)
December 25	Noël (Christmas)

Most shops, banks and government institutions are closed on these days. Banks close the afternoon before a Bank holiday and some banks close on Mondays in the provinces. Good Friday and Boxing Day are not Bank Holidays

1.3 What time is it?

What time is it? _____ Quelle heure est-il?
kehl uhr eh teel?

It's nine o'clock _____ Il est neuf heures
eel eh nuh vuhr

– five past ten _____ Il est dix heures cinq
eel eh dee zuhr sahnk

– a quarter past eleven _ Il est onze heures et quart
eel eh tawnz uhr ay kahr

– twenty past twelve ____ Il est douze heures vingt
eel eh dooz uhr vahn

– half past one _____ Il est une heure et demie
eel eh tewn uhr ay duhmee

– twenty–five to three __	Il est trois heures moins vingt-cinq
	eel eh trwah zuhr mwahn vahn sahnk
– a quarter to four _____	Il est quatre heures moins le quart
	eel eh kahtr uhr mwahn luh kahr
– ten to five _____	Il est cinq heures moins dix
	eel eh sahnk uhr mwahn dees
– twelve noon _____	Il est midi
	eel eh meedee
– midnight _____	Il est minuit
	eel eh meenwee
half an hour_____	une demi-heure
	ewn duhmee uhr
What time? _____	A quelle heure?
	ah kehl uhr?
What time can I come _	A quelle heure puis-je venir?
round?	*ah kehl uhr pwee jhuh vuhneer?*
At... _____	A...
	ah...
After... _____	Après...
	ahpreh...
Before... _____	Avant...
	ahvohn...
Between...and... _____	Entre...et...
	ohntr...ay...
From...to... _____	De...à...
	duh...ah...
In...minutes _____	Dans...minutes
	dohn...meenewt
– an hour _____	Dans une heure
	dohn zewn uhr
– ...hours _____	Dans...heures
	dohn...uhr
– a quarter of an hour _	Dans un quart d'heure
	dohn zuhn kahr duhr
– three quarters of _____	Dans trois quarts d'heure
an hour	*dohn trwah kahr duhr*

early/late	_____	trop tôt/tard
		troa toa/tahr
on time	_____	à temps
		ah tohn
summertime	_____	l'heure d'été
		luhr daytay
wintertime	_____	l'heure d'hiver
		luhr deevehr

1.4 One, two, three...

0	_____	zéro	*zayroa*
1	_____	un	*uhn*
2	_____	deux	*duh*
3	_____	trois	*trwah*
4	_____	quatre	*kahtr*
5	_____	cinq	*sahnk*
6	_____	six	*sees*
7	_____	sept	*seht*
8	_____	huit	*weet*
9	_____	neuf	*nuhf*
10	_____	dix	*dees*
11	_____	onze	*awnz*
12	_____	douze	*dooz*
13	_____	treize	*trehz*
14	_____	quatorze	*kahtorz*
15	_____	quinze	*kahnz*
16	_____	seize	*sehz*
17	_____	dix-sept	*dee seht*
18	_____	dix-huit	*dee zweet*
19	_____	dix-neuf	*deez nuhf*
20	_____	vingt	*vahn*
21	_____	vingt et un	*vahn tay uhn*
22	_____	vingt-deux	*vahn duh*

30	_____	trente	*trohnt*
31	_____	trente et un	*trohn tay uhn*
32	_____	trente-deux	*trohnt duh*
40	_____	quarante	*kahrohnt*
50	_____	cinquante	*sahnkohnt*
60	_____	soixante	*swahssohnt*
70	_____	soixante-dix	*swahssohnt dees*
80	_____	quatre-vingts	*kahtr vahn*
90	_____	quatre-vingt-dix	*kahtr vahn dees*
100	_____	cent	*sohn*
101	_____	cent un	*sohn uhn*
110	_____	cent dix	*sohn dees*
120	_____	cent vingt	*sohn vahn*
200	_____	deux cents	*duh sohn*
300	_____	trois cents	*trwah sohn*
400	_____	quatre cents	*kahtr sohn*
500	_____	cinq cents	*sahnk sohn*
600	_____	six cents	*see sohn*
700	_____	sept cents	*seht sohn*
800	_____	huit cents	*wee sohn*
900	_____	neuf cents	*nuhf sohn*
1,000	_____	mille	*meel*
1,100	_____	mille cent	*meel sohn*
2,000	_____	deux mille	*duh meel*
10,000	_____	dix mille	*dee meel*
100,000	_____	cent mille	*sohn meel*
1,000,000	_____	un million	*uhn meelyawn*
1st	_____	le premier	*luh pruhmyay*
2nd	_____	le deuxième	*luh duhzyehm*
3rd	_____	le troisième	*luh trwahzyehm*
4th	_____	le quatrième	*luh kahtryehm*
5th	_____	le cinquième	*luh sahnkyehm*
6th	_____	le sixième	*luh seezyehm*
7th	_____	le septième	*luh sehtyehm*
8th	_____	le huitième	*luh weetyehm*

9th	le neuvième	*luh nuhvyehm*
10th	le dixième	*luh deezyehm*
11th	le onzième	*luh awnzyehm*
12th	le douzième	*luh doozyehm*
13th	le treizième	*luh trehzyehm*
14th	le quatorzième	*luh kahtorzyehm*
15th	le quinzième	*luh kahnzyehm*
16th	le seizième	*luh sehzyehm*
17th	le dix-septième	*luh dee sehtyehm*
18th	le dix-huitième	*luh dee zweetyehm*
19th	le dix-neuvième	*luh deez nuhvyehm*
20th	le vingtième	*luh vahntyehm*
21st	le vingt et unième	*luh vahn tay-ewnyehm*
22nd	le vingt-deuxième	*luh vahn duhzyehm*
30th	le trentième	*luh trohntyehm*
100th	le centième	*luh sohntyehm*
1,000th	le millième	*luh meelyehm*
once	une fois	*ewn fwah*
twice	deux fois	*duh fwah*
double	le double	*luh doobl*
triple	le triple	*luh treepl*
half	la moitié	*lah mwahtyay*
a quarter	un quart	*uhn kahr*
a third	un tiers	*uhn tyehr*
a couple, a few, some	quelques, un nombre de, quelques *kehlkuh, uhn nawnbr duh, kehlkuh*	
2 + 4 = 6	deux plus quatre égalent six *duh plews kahtr aygahl sees*	
4 - 2 = 2	quatre moins deux égalent deux *kahtr mwahn duh aygahl duh*	
2 x 4 = 8	deux fois quatre égalent huit *duh fwah kahtr aygahl weet*	
4 ÷ 2 = 2	quatre divisé par deux égalent deux *kahtr deeveezay pahr duh aygahl duh*	

odd/even _____	impair/pair
	ahnpehr/pehr
total _____	(au) total
	(oa) totahl
6 x 9 _____	six fois neuf
	see fwah nuhf

1.5 The weather

Is the weather going ___ to be good/bad?	Va-t-il faire beau/mauvais?
	vah teel fehr boa/moaveh?
Is it going to get _____ colder/hotter?	Va-t-il faire plus froid/plus chaud?
	vah teel fehr plew frwah/plew shoa?
What temperature is it __ going to be?	Quelle température va-t-il faire?
	Kehl tohnpayrahtewr vah teel fehr?
Is it going to rain? _____	Va-t-il pleuvoir?
	vah teel pluhvwahr?
Is there going to be a ___ storm?	Va-t-il faire de la tempête?
	vah teel fehr duh lah tohnpeht?
Is it going to snow? ____	Va-t-il neiger?
	vah teel nehjhay?
Is it going to freeze? ___	Va-t-il geler?
	vah teel jhuhlay?
Is the thaw setting in? __	Va-t-il dégeler?
	vah teel dayjhuhlay?
Is it going to be foggy? _	Y aura-t-il du brouillard?
	ee oarah teel dew brooy-yahr?
Is there going to be a ___ thunderstorm?	Va-t-il faire de l'orage?
	vah teel fehr duh lorahjh?
The weather's _____ changing	Le temps change
	luh tohn shohnjh
It's cooling down _____	Ça se rafraîchit
	sah suh rahfrehshee

What's the weather _____
going to be like today/
tomorrow?

Quel temps va-t-il faire
aujourd'hui/demain?
*kehl tohn vah teel fehr
oajhoordwee/duhmahn?*

nuageux cloudy	pluvieux raining	les rafales de vent squalls
beau fine	la canicule scorching hot	l'ouragan (m.) hurricane
chaud hot	la grêle hail	lourd muggy
...degrés (au-dessous/au- dessus de zéro) ...degrees (below/ above zero)	la neige snow	l'orage (m.) thunderstorm
	la pluie rain	orageux stormy
couvert overcast	la vague de chaleur heatwave	pénétrant bleak
le crachin drizzle	l'averse (f.) shower	ciel dégagé clear
doux mild	le brouillard fog	brumeux misty
ensoleillé sunny	le gel ice	vent faible/ modéré/fort
frais chilly	le vent wind	light/moderate/ strong wind
froid cold	le verglas black ice	venteux windy
humide damp	les nuages clouds	

1.6 Here, there...

See also 5.1 Asking for directions

here/there _____	ici/là
	eesee/lah
somewhere/nowhere ___	quelque part/nulle part
	kehlkuh pahr/newl pahr
everywhere _____	partout
	pahrtoo
far away/nearby _____	loin/à côté
	lwahn/ah koatay
right/left _____	la droite/la gauche
	lah drwaht/lah goash
to the right/left of _____	à droite de/à gauche de
	ah drwaht duh/ah goash duh
straight ahead _____	tout droit
	too drwah
via _____	par
	pahr
in _____	dans
	dohn
on _____	sur
	sewr
under _____	sous
	soo
against _____	contre
	kawntr
opposite _____	en face de
	ohn fahs duh
next to _____	à côté de
	ah koatay duh
near _____	près de
	preh duh
in front of _____	devant
	devohn

in the centre	au milieu de
	oa meelyuh duh
forward	en avant
	ohn nahvohn
down	en bas
	ohn bah
up	en haut
	ohn oa
inside	à l'intérieur
	ah lahntayryuhr
outside	à l'extérieur
	ah lehxtayryuhr
behind	derrière
	dehryehr
at the front	à l'avant
	ah lahvohn
at the back	à l'arrière
	ah lahryehr
in the north	au nord
	oa nor
to the south	vers le sud
	vehr luh sewd
from the west	venant de l'ouest
	vuhnohn duh lwehst
from the east	venant de l'est
	vuhnohn duh lehst

1.7 What does that sign say?

See also 5.4 Traffic signs

à louer
for hire

à vendre
for sale

accueil
reception

animaux interdits
no pets allowed

ascenseur
lift

attention à la
  marche
mind the step

attention chien
  méchant
beware of the dog

caisse
pay here

complet
full

dames
ladies

danger
danger

défense de toucher
please do not touch

eau non potable
no drinking water

en panne
out of order

entrée
entrance

entrée gratuite
admission free

entrée interdite
no entry

escalier roulant
escalator

escalier
stairs

escalier de secours
fire escape

...étage
...floor

frein de secours
emergency brake

haute tension
high voltage

heures d'ouverture
opening hours

interdit d'allumer un
  feu
no open fires

interdit de fumer
no smoking

interdit de
  photographier
no photographs

liquidation de stock
closing-down sale

messieurs
gents/gentlemen

ne pas déranger s'il
  vous plaît
do not disturb please

ouvert/fermé
open/closed

peinture fraîche
wet paint

pelouse interdite
keep off the grass

premiers soins
first aid

propriété privée
private (property)

renseignements
information

réservé
reserved

risque d'incendie
fire hazard

soldes
sale

sortie
exit

sortie de secours
emergency exit

pousser/tirer
push/pull

toilettes, wc
toilets

1.8 Telephone alphabet

a	ah	comme Anatole	*kom ahnnahtol*
b	bay	comme Berthe	*kom behrt*
c	say	comme Célestin	*kom saylehstahn*
d	day	comme Désiré	*kom dayzeeray*
e	uh	comme Eugène	*kom uhjhehn*
f	ehf	comme François	*kom frohnswah*
g	jhay	comme Gaston	*kom gahstawn*
h	ash	comme Henri	*kom ohnree*
i	ee	comme Irma	*kom eermah*
j	jhee	comme Joseph	*kom jhosehf*
k	kah	comme Kléber	*kom klaybehr*
l	ehl	comme Louis	*kom looee*
m	ehm	comme Marcel	*kom mahrsehl*
n	ehn	comme Nicolas	*kom neekolah*
o	oh	comme Oscar	*kom oskahr*
p	pay	comme Pierre	*kom pyehr*
q	kew	comme Quintal	*kom kahntahl*
r	ehr	comme Raoul	*kom rahool*
s	ehs	comme Suzanne	*kom sewzahnn*
t	tay	comme Thérèse	*kom tayrehz*
u	ew	comme Ursule	*kom ewrsewl*
v	vee	comme Victor	*kom veektor*
w	doobluhvay	comme William	*kom weelyahm*
x	eex	comme Xavier	*kom gsahvyay*
y	eegrehk	comme Yvonne	*kom eevon*
z	zehd	comme Zoé	*kom zoa-ay*

1.9 Personal details

surname_____ nom
nawn

christian name(s) _____ prénom(s)
praynawn

initials _____ initiales
eeneesyahl

address _____ adresse (rue/numéro)
  (street/number) *ahdrehs (rew/newmayroa)*

post code/town _____ code postal/ville
kod postahl/veel

sex (male/female)_____ sexe (m/f)
sehx (ehm/ehf)

nationality _____ nationalité
nahsyonahleetay

date of birth_____ date de naissance
daht duh nehsohns

place of birth_____ lieu de naissance
lyuh duh nehsohns

occupation _____ profession
profehsyawn

married/single/ _____ marié(e) /célibataire/divorcé(e)
  divorced *mahreeay/sayleebahtehr/deevorsay*

widowed _____ veuf/veuve
vuhf/vuhv

(number of) children____ (nombre d')enfants
(nawnbr d)ohnfohn

identity card/passport/ _ numéro de carte d'identité/
  driving licence number   passeport/permis de conduire
newmayroa duh kahrt deedohnteetay/
pahspor/pehrmee duh kawndweer

place and date of_____ lieu et date de délivrance
  issue *lyuh ay daht duh dayleevrohns*

23

2
Courtesies

● **It is usual in France** to shake hands on meeting and parting company. Female friends and relatives may kiss each other on both cheeks when meeting and parting company. With men this varies according to the region. It is also polite to say monsieur and madame quite systematically as part of a greeting, i.e. Bonjour, monsieur; au revoir, madame.

● **The English** 'you' is expressed in French by either 'tu' or 'vous'. 'Tu' is the more familiar form of address, used to talk to someone close or used between young people or when adults are talking to young children. 'Vous' is the more formal and polite form of address. 'On' is the generalised form of 'nous' meaning people in general ('one' and 'we' in English).

2.1 Greetings

Hello, Mr Smith_____	Bonjour monsieur Smith *bawnjhoor muhsyuh dewpawn*
Hello, Mrs Jones _____	Bonjour madame Jones *bawnjhoor mahdahm dewrohn*
Hello, Peter _____	Salut, Pierre *sahlew, pyehr*
Hi, Helen _____	Ça va, Hélène? *sah vah, aylehn?*
Good morning, madam_	Bonjour madame *bawnjhoor mahdahm*
Good afternoon, sir ____	Bonjour monsieur *bawnjhoor muhsyuh*
Good evening _____	Bonsoir *bawhnswahr*
How are you? _____	Comment allez-vous? *komohn tahlay voo?*
Fine, thank you, _____ and you?	Très bien et vous? *treh byahn ay voo?*
Very well_____	Très bien *treh byahn*

Not very well	Pas très bien
	pah treh byahn
Not too bad	Ça va
	sah vah
I'd better be going	Je m'en vais
	jhuh mohn veh
I have to be going	Je dois partir
	jhuh dwah pahrteer
Someone's waiting for me	On m'attend
	awn mahtohn
Bye!	Salut!
	sahlew!
Goodbye	Au revoir
	oa ruhvwahr
See you soon	A bientôt
	ah byahntoa
See you later	A tout à l'heure
	ah too tah luhr
See you in a little while	A tout de suite
	ah toot sweet
Sleep well	Dormez bien/dors bien
	dormay byahn, dor byahn
Good night	Bonne nuit
	bon nwee
Have fun	Amuse-toi bien
	ahmewz twah byahn
Good luck	Bonne chance
	bon shahns
Have a nice holiday	Bonnes vacances
	bon vahkohns
Have a good trip	Bon voyage
	bawn vwahyahjh
Thank you, you too	Merci, de même
	mehrsee, duh mehm
Say hello to...for me	Mes amitiés à...
	may zahmeetyay ah...

2.2 How to ask a question

Who? _____	Qui?
	kee?
Who's that? _____	Qui est-ce?
	kee ehs?
What? _____	Quoi?
	kwah?
What's there to _____	Qu'est-ce qu'on peut voir ici?
see here?	*kehsk awn puh vwahr eesee?*
What kind of hotel _____	C'est quelle sorte d'hôtel?
is that?	*seh kehl sort doatehl?*
Where? _____	Où?
	oo?
Where's the toilet? _____	Où sont les toilettes?
	oo sawn lay twahleht?
Where are you going? __	Où allez-vous?
	oo ahlay voo?
Where are you from? ___	D'où venez-vous?
	doo vuhnay voo?
How? _____	Comment?
	komohn?
How far is that? _____	C'est loin?
	seh lwahn?
How long does that ___	Combien de temps faut-il?
take?	*kawnbyahn duh tohn foa teel?*
How long is the trip? ___	Combien de temps dure le voyage?
	kawnbyahn duh tohn dewr luh vwahyahjh?
How much? _____	Combien?
	kawnbyahn?
How much is this? _____	C'est combien?
	seh kawnbyahn?
What time is it? _____	Quelle heure est-il?
	kehl uhr eh teel?
Which? _____	Quel? Quels?/Quelle? Quelles?
	kehl?

Which glass is mine?	Quel est mon verre?
	kehl eh mawn vehr?
When?	Quand?
	kohn?
When are you leaving?	Quand partez-vous?
	kohn pahrtay voo?
Why?	Pourquoi?
	poorkwah?
Could you...me?	Pouvez-vous me...?
	poovay voo muh...?
Could you help me, please?	Pouvez-vous m'aider s'il vous plaît?
	poovay voo mayday seel voo pleh?
Could you point that out to me?	Pouvez-vous me l'indiquer?
	poovay voo muh lahndeekay?
Could you come with me, please?	Pouvez-vous m'accompagner s'il vous plaît?
	poovay voo mahkawnpahnnyay seel voo pleh?
Could you...?	Voulez-vous...?
	voolay voo...?
Could you reserve some tickets for me, please?	Voulez-vous me réserver des places s'il vous plaît?
	voolay voo muh rayzehrvay day plahs seel voo pleh?
Do you know...?	Connaissez-vous...?
	konehssay voo...?
Do you know another hotel, please?	Vous connaissez peut-être un autre hôtel?
	voo konehssay puh tehtr uhn noatr oatehl?
Do you know whether...?	Savez-vous si...?
	sahvay voo see...?
Do you have a...?	Avez-vous un...?
	ahvay voo zuhn...?
Do you have a vegetarian dish, please?	Vous avez peut-être un plat sans viande?
	voo zahvay puh tehtr uhn plah sohn vyohnd?

28

I'd like...	Je voudrais...
	jhuh voodreh...
I'd like a kilo of apples, please	Je voudrais un kilo de pommes
	jhuh voodreh zuhn keeloa duh pom
Can I...?	Puis-je...?
	pwee jhuh...?
Can I take this?	Puis-je prendre ceci?
	pwee jhuh prohndr suhsee?
Can I smoke here?	Puis-je fumer ici?
	pwee jhuh fewmay eesee?
Could I ask you something?	Puis-je vous demander quelque chose?
	pwee jhuh voo duhmohnday kehlkuh shoaz?

2.3 How to reply

Yes, of course	Oui, bien sûr
	wee, byahn sewr
No, I'm sorry	Non, je suis désolé
	nawn, jhuh swee dayzolay
Yes, what can I do for you?	Oui, que puis-je faire pour vous?
	wee, kuh pwee jhuh fehr poor voo?
Just a moment, please	Un moment s'il vous plaît
	uhn momohn seel voo pleh
No, I don't have time now	Non, je n'ai pas le temps en ce moment
	nawn, jhuh nay pah luh tohn ohn suh momohn
No, that's impossible	Non, c'est impossible
	nawn, seh tahnposseebl
I think so	Je le crois bien
	jhuh luh krwah byahn
I agree	Je le pense aussi
	jhuh luh pohns oasee
I hope so too	Je l'espère aussi
	jhuh lehspehr oasee

No, not at all _____	Non, absolument pas
	nawn, ahbsolewmohn pah
No, no-one _____	Non, personne
	nawn, pehrson
No, nothing _____	Non, rien
	nawn, ryahn
That's (not) right _____	C'est (ce n'est pas) exact
	seht (suh neh pahz) ehgzah
I (don't) agree _____	Je suis (je ne suis pas) d'accord avec vous
	jhuh swee (jhuh nuh swee pah) dahkor ahvehk voo
All right_____	C'est bien *seh byahn*
Okay _____	D'accord *dahkor*
Perhaps _____	Peut-être *puh tehtr*
I don't know _____	Je ne sais pas *jhuh nuh seh pah*

2.4 Thank you

Thank you _____	Merci/merci bien
	mehrsee/mehrsee byahn
You're welcome _____	De rien/avec plaisir
	duh ryahn/ahvehk playzeer
Thank you very much __	Merci beaucoup
	mehrsee boakoo
Very kind of you _____	C'est aimable de votre part
	seh taymahbl duh votr pahr
I enjoyed it very much__	C'était un réel plaisir
	sayteh tuhn rayehl playzeer
Thank you for your_____ trouble	Je vous remercie pour la peine
	jhuh voo ruhmehrsee poor lah pehn
You shouldn't have _____	Vous n'auriez pas dû
	voo noaryay pah dew
That's all right _____	Pas de problème
	pah duh problehm

2.5 Sorry

Excuse me_____	Excusez-moi
	ehxkewzay mwah
Sorry! _____	Pardon! *pahrdawn!*
I'm sorry, I didn't _____ know...	Pardon, je ne savais pas que...
	pahrdawn jhuh nuh sahveh pah kuh...
I do apologise_____	Excusez-moi
	ehxkewzay mwah
I'm sorry_____	Je suis désolé
	jhuh swee dayzolay
I didn't do it on _____ purpose, it was an accident	Je ne l'ai pas fait exprès, c'était un accident
	jhuh ne lay pah feh ehxpreh, sayteh tuhn nahxeedohn
That's all right _____	Ce n'est pas grave
	suh neh pah grahv
Never mind _____	Ça ne fait rien
	sah nuh feh ryahn
It could've happened___ to anyone	Ça peut arriver à tout le monde
	sah puh ahreevay ah too luh mawnd

2.6 What do you think?

Which do you prefer? __	Qu'est-ce que vous préférez?
	kehs kuh voo prayfayray?
What do you think? ____	Qu'en penses-tu?
	kohn pohns tew?
Don't you like _____ dancing?	Tu n'aimes pas danser?
	tew nehm pah dohnsay?
I don't mind_____	Ça m'est égal *sah meh taygahl*
Well done! _____	Très bien! *treh byahn!*
Not bad!_____	Pas mal! *pah mahl!*
Great! _____	Génial! *jhaynyahl!*
Wonderful! _____	Super! *sewpehr!*

It's really nice here! _____ C'est drôlement agréable ici!
seh droalmohn ahgrayahbl eesee!

How nice! _____ Pas mal, chouette!
pah mahl, shweht!

How nice for you! _____ C'est formidable!
seh formeedahbl!

I'm (not) very happy _____ Je suis (ne suis pas) très satisfait(e) de...
with... *jhuh swee (nuh swee pah) treh*
sahteesfeh(t) duh...

I'm glad... _____ Je suis content(e) que...
jhuh swee kawntohn(t) kuh...

I'm having a great time _ Je m'amuse beaucoup
jhuh mahmewz boakoo

I'm looking forward _____ Je m'en réjouis
to it *jhuh mohn rayjhwee*

I hope it'll work out _____ J'espère que cela réussira
jhehspehr kuh suhlah rayewseerah

That's ridiculous! _____ C'est nul! *seh newl!*

That's terrible! _____ Quelle horreur! *kehl oruhr!*

What a pity! _____ C'est dommage! *seh domahjh!*

That's filthy! _____ C'est dégoûtant!
seh daygootohn!

What a load of _____ C'est ridicule/C'est absurde!
rubbish! *seh reedeekewl/seh tahbsewrd!*

I don't like... _____ Je n'aime pas...
jhuh nehm pah...

I'm bored to death _____ Je m'ennuie à mourir
jhuh mohnnwee ah mooreer

I've had enough _____ J'en ai assez/ras le bol
jhohn nay ahsay/rahl bol

This is no good _____ Ce n'est pas possible
suh neh pah posseebl

I was expecting _____ Je m'attendais à quelque chose de très
something completely différent
different *jhuh mahtohndeh ah kehlkuh shoaz duh*
treh deefayrohn

3.1 I beg your pardon?

I don't speak any/ _____ I speak a little...	Je ne parle pas/je parle un peu... *jhuh nuh pahrl pah/jhuh pahrl uhn puh..*
I'm English_____	Je suis anglais/anglaise *jhuh swee zohngleh/zohnglehz*
I'm Scottish_____	Je suis écossais/écossaise *jhuh swee zaykosseh/zaykossehz*
I'm Irish _____	Je suis irlandais/irlandaise *jhuh swee zeerlohndeh/zeerlohndehz*
I'm Welsh_____	Je suis gallois/galloise *jhuh swee gahlwah/gahlwahz*
Do you speak _____ English/French/ German?	Parlez-vous anglais/français/allemand? *pahrlay voo ohngleh/ frohnseh/ahlmohn?*
Is there anyone who ___ speaks...?	Y a-t-il quelqu'un qui parle...? *ee yah teel kehlkuhn kee pahrl...?*
I beg your pardon? ____	Que dites-vous? *kuh deet voo?*
I (don't) understand ____	Je (ne) comprends (pas) *jhuh (nuh) kawnprohn (pah)*
Do you understand me?	Me comprenez-vous? *me kawnpruhnay voo?*
Could you repeat that, _ please?	Voulez-vous répéter s'il vous plaît? *voolay voo raypaytay seel voo pleh?*
Could you speak more _ slowly, please?	Pouvez-vous parler plus lentement? *poovay voo pahrlay plew lohntmohn?*
What does that word___ mean?	Qu'est-ce que ce mot veut dire? *kehs kuh suh moa vuh deer?*
Is that similar to/the____ same as...?	Est-ce (environ) la même chose que...? *ehs (ohnveerawn) lah mehm shoaz kuh...?*
Could you write that ___ down for me, please?	Pouvez-vous me l'écrire? *poovay voo muh laykreer?*
Could you spell that ___ for me, please?	Pouvez-vous me l'épeler? *poovay voo muh laypuhlay?*

(See 1.8 Telephone alphabet)

Could you point that ___
out in this phrase
book, please?

Pouvez-vous me le montrer dans ce
guide de conversation?
*poovay voo muh luh mawntray dohn suh
gueed duh kawnvehrsahsyawn?*

One moment, please, ___
I have to look it up

Un moment, je dois le chercher
uhn momohn, jhuh dwah luh shehrshay

I can't find the word/the
sentence

Je ne trouve pas le mot/la phrase
jhuh nuh troov pah luh moa/lah frahz

How do you say _____
that in...?

Comment dites-vous cela en...?
komohn deet voo suhlah ohn...?

How do you _____
pronounce that?

Comment prononcez-vous cela?
komohn pronawnsay voo suhlah?

3.2 Introductions

May I introduce myself?

Puis-je me présenter?
pwee jhuh muh prayzohntay?

My name's... _____

Je m'appelle...
jhuh mahpehl...

I'm... _____

Je suis...
jhuh swee...

What's your name? ____

Comment vous appelez-vous?
komohn voo zahpuhlay voo?

May I introduce...? _____

Puis-je vous présenter?
pwee jhuh voo prayzohntay?

This is my wife/ _____
daughter/mother/
girlfriend

Voici ma femme/fille/mère/mon amie
*vwahsee mah fahm/feey/mehr/mawn
nahmee*

– my husband/son/ ____
father/boyfriend

Voici mon mari/fils/père/ami
vwahsee mawn mahree/fees/pehr/ahmee

How do you do_____

Enchanté(e).
ohnshohntay

Pleased to meet you ___ Je suis heureux(se) de faire votre
   connaissance
   jhuh swee zuhruh(z) duh fehr votr
   kohnehssohns
Where are you from? ___ D'où venez-vous?
   doo vuhnay voo?
I'm from _____ Je viens
England/Scotland/   d'Angleterre/d'Ecosse/d'Irlande/du pays
Ireland/Wales   de Galles
   jhuh vyahn dohngluhtehr/daykos/deerlohnd
   dew payee duh gahl
What city do you live __ Vous habitez dans quelle ville?
in?   *voo zahbeetay dohn kehl veel?*
In..., It's near... _____ A...C'est à côté de...
   ah...seh tah koatay duh...
Have you been here ___ Etes-vous ici depuis longtemps?
long?   *eht voo zeesee duhpwee lawntohn?*
A few days_____ Depuis quelques jours
   depwee kehlkuh jhoor
How long are you_____ Combien de temps restez-vous ici?
staying here?   *kawnbyahn duh tohn rehstay voo zeesee?*
We're (probably) leaving Nous partirons (probablement)
tomorrow/in two   demain/dans quinze jours
weeks   *noo pahrteerawn (probahbluhmohn)*
   duhmahn/dohn kahnz jhoor
Where are you staying? Où logez-vous?
   oo lojhay voo?
In a hotel/an apartment_ Dans un hôtel/appartement
   dohn zuhn noatehl/ahpahrtuhmohn
On a camp site_____ Dans un camping
   dohn zuhn kohnpeeng
With friends/relatives ___ Chez des amis/chez de la famille
   shay day zahmee/shay duh lah fahmeey
Are you here on your___ Etes-vous ici seul/avec votre famille?
own/with your family?   *eht voo zeesee suhl/ahvehk votr fahmeey?*
I'm on my own _____ Je suis seul(e)
   jhuh swee suhl

I'm with my _____ partner/wife/husband	Je suis avec mon ami(e)/ma femme/mon mari *jhuh swee zahvehk mawn nahmee/mah fahm/mawn mahree*
– with my family _____	Je suis avec ma famille *jhuh swee zahvehk mah fahmeey*
– with relatives _____	Je suis avec de la famille *jhuh swee zahvehk duh lah fahmeey*
– with a friend/friends __	Je suis avec un ami/une amie /des amis *jhuh swee zahvehk uhn nahmee/ewn ahmee/day zahmee*
Are you married? _____	Etes-vous marié(e)? *eht voo mahreeay?*
Do you have a steady __ boyfriend/girlfriend?	As-tu un petit ami (une petite amie)? *ah tew uhn puhtee tahmee (ewn puhteet ahmee)?*
That's none of your ____ business	Cela ne vous regarde pas *suhlah nuh voo ruhgahrd pah*
I'm married _____	Je suis marié(e) *jhuh swee mahreeay*
– single_____	Je suis célibataire *jhuh swee sayleebahtehr*
– separated _____	Je suis séparé(e) *jhuh swee saypahray*
– divorced _____	Je suis divorcé(e) *jhuh swee deevorsay*
– a widow/widower ____	Je suis veuf/veuve *jhuh swee vuhf/vuhv*
I live alone/with_____ someone	J'habite tout(e) seul(e)/avec quelqu'un *jhahbeet too suhl(toot suhl)/ahvehk kehlkuhn*
Do you have any _____ children/ grandchildren?	Avez-vous des enfants/petits-enfants? *ahvay voo day zohnfohn/puhtee zohnfohn?*
How old are you?_____	Quel âge avez-vous? *kehl ahjh ahvay voo?*

How old is he/she? ____	Quel âge a-t-il/a-t-elle?
	kehl ahjh ah teel/ah tehl?
I'm...years old _____	J'ai...ans
	jhay...ohn
He's/she's...years old __	Il/elle a...ans
	eel/ehl ah...ohn
What do you do for a __ living?	Quel est votre métier?
	kehl eh votr maytyay?
I work in an office_____	Je travaille dans un bureau
	jhuh trahvahy dohn zuhn bewroa
I'm a student/ _____ I'm at school	Je fais des études/je vais à l'école
	jhuh feh day zaytewd/jhuh veh zah laykol
I'm unemployed _____	Je suis au chômage
	jhuh swee zoa shoamajh
I'm retired _____	Je suis retraité(e)
	jhuh swee ruhtrehtay
I'm on a disability_____ pension	Je suis en invalidité
	jhuh swee zohn nahnvahleedeetay
I'm a housewife _____	Je suis femme au foyer
	jhuh swee fahm oa fwahyay
Do you like your job? __	Votre travail vous plaît?
	votr trahvahy voo pleh?
Most of the time_____	Ça dépend
	sah daypohn
I prefer holidays _____	J'aime mieux les vacances
	Jhehm myuh lay vahkohns

3.3 Starting/ending a conversation

Could I ask you _____ something?	Puis-je vous poser une question?
	pwee jhuh voo poazay ewn kehstyawn?
Excuse me_____	Excusez-moi
	ehxkewsay mwah
Excuse me, could you__ help me?	Pardon, pouvez-vous m'aider?
	pahrdawn, poovay voo mayday?

Yes, what's the _____ problem?	Oui, qu'est-ce qui se passe? *wee, kehs kee suh pahss?*
What can I do for you? _	Que puis-je faire pour vous? *kuh pwee jhuh fehr poor voo?*
Sorry, I don't have time_ now	Excusez-moi, je n'ai pas le temps maintenant *ehxkewzay mwah, jhuh nay pah luh tohn mahntuhnohn*
Do you have a light? ___	Vous avez du feu? *voo zahvay dew fuh?*
May I join you? _____	Puis-je m'asseoir à côté de vous? *pwee jhuh mahsswahr ah koatay duh voo?*
Could you take a _____ picture of me/us? Press this button.	Voulez-vous me/nous prendre en photo? Appuyez sur ce bouton. *voolay voo muh/noo prohndr ohn foatoa? ahpweeyay sewr suh bootawn*
Leave me alone _____	Laissez-moi tranquille *laysay mwah trohnkeey*
Get lost _____	Fichez le camp *feeshay luh kohn*
Go away or I'll scream _	Si vous ne partez pas, je crie *see voo nuh pahrtay pah, jhuh kree*

3.4 Congratulations and condolences

Happy birthday/many __ happy returns	Bon anniversaire/bonne fête *bohn nahnneevehrsehr/bon feht*
Please accept my _____ condolences	Mes condoléances *may kawndolayohns*
I'm very sorry for you __	Cela me peine beaucoup pour vous *suhlah muh pehn boakoo poor voo*

3.5 A chat about the weather

See also 1.5 The weather

It's so hot/cold today! __	Qu'est-ce qu'il fait chaud/froid aujourd'hui!
	kehs keel feh shoa/frwah oajhoordwee!
Nice weather, isn't it? __	Il fait beau, n'est-ce pas?
	eel feh boa, nehs pah?
What a wind/storm! ____	Quel vent/orage!
	kehl vohn/orahjh!
All that rain/snow! _____	Quelle pluie/neige!
	kehl plwee/nehjh!
All that fog! _____	Quel brouillard!
	kehl brooy-yahr!
Has the weather been__ like this for long here?	Fait-il ce temps-là depuis longtemps?
	feh teel suh tohn lah duhpwee lawntohn?
Is it always this _____ hot/cold here?	Fait-il toujours aussi chaud/froid ici?
	feh teel toojhoor oasee shoa/frwah eesee?
Is it always this _____ dry/wet here?	Fait-il toujours aussi sec/humide ici?
	feh teel toojhoor oasee sehk/ewmeed eesee?

3.6 Hobbies

Do you have any _____ hobbies?	Avez-vous des passe-temps?
	ahvay voo day pahs tohn?
I like painting/ _____ reading/photography/ DIY	J'aime peindre/lire/la photo/le bricolage
	jhehm pahndr/leer/lah foatoa/luh breekolahjh
I like music _____	J'aime la musique
	jhehm lah mewzeek
I like playing the _____ guitar/piano	J'aime jouer de la guitare/du piano
	jhehm jhooay duh lah gueetahr/dew pyahnoa

I like going to the _____ movies	J'aime aller au cinéma
	jhehm ahlay oa seenaymah
I like travelling/ _____ sport/fishing/walking	J'aime voyager/faire du sport/la pêche/me promener
	jhehm vwahyahjhay/fehr dew spor/lah pehsh/ muh promuhnay

3.7 Being the host(ess)

See also 4 Eating out

Can I offer you a _____ drink?	Puis-je vous offrir quelque chose à boire?
	pwee jhuh voo zofreer kehlkuh shoaz ah bwahr?
What would you like ___ to drink?	Que désires-tu boire?
	kuh dayzeer tew bwahr?
Something non- _____ alcoholic, please.	De préférence quelque chose sans alcool
	duh prayfayrohns kehlkuh shoaz sohn zahlkol
Would you like a_____ cigarette/cigar/to roll your own?	Voulez-vous une cigarette/un cigare/rouler une cigarette?
	voolay voo zewn seegahreht/uhn seegahr/roolay ewn seegahreht?
I don't smoke _____	Je ne fume pas
	jhuh nuh fewm pah

3.8 Invitations

Are you doing anything_ tonight?	Faites-vous quelque chose ce soir?
	feht voo kehlkuh shoaz suh swahr?
Do you have any plans _ for today/this afternoon/tonight?	Avez-vous déjà fait des projets pour aujourd'hui/cet après-midi/ce soir?
	ahvay voo dayjhah feh day projheh poor oa-jhoordwee/seht ahpreh meedee/suh swahr?

Would you like to go ___ out with me?	Aimeriez-vous sortir avec moi?
	aymuhryay voo sorteer ahvehk mwah?
Would you like to go ___ dancing with me?	Aimeriez-vous aller danser avec moi?
	aymuhryay voo zahlay dohnsay ahvehk mwah?
Would you like to have _ lunch/dinner with me?	Aimeriez-vous déjeuner/dîner avec moi?
	aymuhryay voo dayjhuhnay/deenay ahvehk mwah?
Would you like to _____ come to the beach with me?	Aimeriez-vous aller à la plage avec moi?
	aymuhryay voo zahlay ah lah plahjh ahvehk mwah?
Would you like to _____ come into town with us?	Aimeriez-vous aller en ville avec nous?
	aymuhryay voo zahlay ohn veel ahvehk noo?
Would you like to _____ come and see some friends with us?	Aimeriez-vous aller chez des amis avec nous?
	aymuhryay voo zahlay shay day zahmee ahvehk noo?
Shall we dance?_____	On danse?
	awn dohns?
– sit at the bar? _____	On va s'asseoir au bar?
	awn vah saswahr oa bahr?
– get something to ____ drink?	On va boire quelque chose?
	awn vah bwahr kehlkuh shoaz?
– go for a walk/drive? __	On va marcher un peu/on va faire un tour en voiture?
	awn vah mahrshay uhn puh/awn vah fehr uhn toor ohn vwahtewr?
Yes, all right_____	Oui, d'accord
	wee, dahkor
Good idea _____	Bonne idée
	bon eeday
No (thank you) _____	Non (merci)
	nawn (mehrsee)
Maybe later _____	Peut-être tout à l'heure
	puh tehtr too tah luhr

I don't feel like it_____	Je n'en ai pas envie *jhuh nohn nay pah zohnvee*
I don't have time _____	Je n'ai pas le temps *jhuh nay pah luh tohn*
I already have a date___	J'ai déjà un autre rendez-vous *jhay dayjhah uhn noatr rohnday voo*
I'm not very good at dancing/volleyball/ swimming	Je ne sais pas danser/jouer au volley/nager *jhuh nuh seh pah dohnsay/jhooay oa volay/nahjhay*

3.9 Paying a compliment

You look wonderful!_____	Vous avez l'air en pleine forme! *voo zahvay lehr ohn plehn form!*
I like your car! _____	Quelle belle voiture! *kehl behl vwahtewr!*
I like your ski outfit! ____	Quelle belle combinaison de ski! *kehl behl kawnbeenehzawn duh skee!*
You're a nice boy/girl___	Tu es un garçon/une fille sympathique *tew eh zuhn gahrsohn/ewn feey sahnpahteek*
What a sweet child! ____	Quel adorable enfant! *kehl ahdorahbl ohnfohn!*
You're a wonderful_____ dancer!	Vous dansez très bien! *voo dohnsay treh byahn!*
You're a wonderful_____ cook!	Vous faites très bien la cuisine! *voo feht treh byahn lah kweezeen!*
You're a terrific soccer _ player!	Vous jouez très bien au football! *voo jhooay treh byahn oa footbol!*

3.10 Chatting someone up

I like being with you____	J'aime bien être près de toi
	jhehm byahn ehtr preh duh twah
I've missed you so ____ much	Tu m'as beaucoup manqué
	tew mah boakoo mohnkay
I dreamt about you ____	J'ai rêvé de toi
	jhay rehvay duh twah
I think about you all day	Je pense à toi toute la journée
	jhuh pohns ah twah toot lah jhoornay
You have such a sweet_ smile	Tu souris si gentiment
	tew sooree see jhohnteemohn
You have such beautiful eyes	Tu as de si jolis yeux
	tew ah duh see jhoalee zyuh
I'm in love with you ____	Je suis amoureux/se de toi
	jhuh swee zahmooruh(z) duh twah
I'm in love with you too_	Moi aussi de toi
	mwah oasee duh twah
I love you_____	Je t'aime
	jhuh tehm
I love you too _____	Je t'aime aussi
	jhuh tehm oasee
I don't feel as strongly__ about you	Je n'ai pas d'aussi forts sentiments pour toi
	jhuh nay pah doasee for sohnteemohn poor twah
I already have a _____ boyfriend/girlfriend	J'ai déjà un ami/une amie
	jhay dayjhah uhn nahmee/ewn ahmee
I'm not ready for that___	Je n'en suis pas encore là
	jhuh nohn swee pah zohnkor lah
This is going too fast___ for me.	Ça va un peu trop vite
	sah vah uhn puh troa veet
Take your hands off me	Ne me touche pas
	nuh muh toosh pah

Okay, no problem_____	D'accord, pas de problème
	dahkor, pah duh problehm
Will you stay with me __ tonight?	Tu restes avec moi cette nuit?
	tew rehst ahvehk mwah seht nwee?
I'd like to go to bed ____ with you	J'aimerais coucher avec toi
	jhehmuhreh kooshay ahvehk twah
Only if we use a _____ condom	Seulement en utilisant un préservatif
	suhlmohn ohn newteeleezohn uhn prayzehrvahteef
We have to be careful __ about AIDS	Il faut être prudent à cause du sida
	eel foa tehtr prewdohn ah koaz dew seedah
That's what they all say	Ils disent tous pareil
	eel deez toos pahrehy
We shouldn't take any__ risks	Ne prenons aucun risque
	nuh pruhnawn zoakuhn reesk
Do you have a condom? _____	Tu as un préservatif?
	tew ah zuhn prayzehrvahteef?
No? In that case we ___ won't do it	Non? Alors je ne veux pas
	nawn? ahlor jhuh nuh vuh pah

3.11 Arrangements

When will I see _____ you again?	Quand est-ce que je te revois?
	kohn tehs kuh jhuh tuh ruhvwah?
Are you free over the ___ weekend?	Vous êtes/tu es libre ce week-end?
	voozeht/tew eh leebr suh week-ehnd?
What shall we _____ arrange?	Que décidons-nous?
	kuh dayseedawn noo?
Where shall we meet?__	Où nous retrouvons-nous?
	oo noo ruhtroovawn noo?
Will you pick me/us up?	Vous venez me/nous chercher?
	voo vuhnay muh/noo shehrshay?
Shall I pick you up?____	Je viens vous/te chercher?
	jhuh vyahn voo/tuh shehrshay?

| I have to be home by... | Je dois être à la maison à...heures |
| | *jhuh dwah zehtr ah lah mehzawn ah...uhr* |

3.12 Saying goodbye

I don't want to see you anymore	Je ne veux plus vous revoir
	jhuh nuh vuh plew voo ruhvwahr
Can I take you home?	Puis-je vous raccompagner à la maison?
	pwee jhuh voo rahkawnpahnyay ah lah mehzawn?
Can I write/call you?	Puis-je vous écrire/téléphoner?
	pwee jhuh voo zaykreer/taylayfonay?
Will you write/call me?	M'écrirez-vous/me téléphonerez-vous?
	maykreeray voo/muh taylayfonuhray voo?
Can I have your address/phone number?	Puis-je avoir votre adresse/numéro de téléphone?
	pwee jhahvwahr votr ahdrehs/newmayroa duh taylayfon?
Thanks for everything	Merci pour tout
	mehrsee poor too
It was very nice	C'était très agréable
	sayteh treh zahgrayahbl
Say hello to...	Présentez mes amitiés à...
	prayzohntay may zahmeetyay ah...
Good luck	Bonne chance
	bon shohns
When will you be back?	Quand est-ce que tu reviens?
	kohn tehs kuh tew ruhvyahn?
I'll be waiting for you	Je t'attendrai
	jhuh tahtohndray
I'd like to see you again	J'aimerais te revoir
	jhehmuhreh tuh ruhvwahr

| I hope we meet
   again soon | J'espère que nous nous reverrons bientôt
jhehspehr kuh noo noo ruhvehrawn
   byahntoa |
| You are welcome _____ | Vous êtes le/la bienvenu(e)
voozeht luh/lah byahnvuhnew |

4

Eating out

● **In France** people usually have three meals:

1 *Le petit déjeuner* (breakfast) approx. between 7.30 and 10am. Breakfast is light and consists of *café au lait* (white coffee) or lemon tea, a croissant, or slices of baguette (French bread), with butter and jam.

2 *Le déjeuner* (lunch) approx. between midday and 2pm. Lunch always includes a hot dish and is the most important meal of the day. Offices and shops often close and lunch is taken at home, in a restaurant or canteen (in some factories and schools). It usually consists of four courses:

– starter
– main course
– cheese
– dessert

3 *Le dîner* (dinner) between 7.30 and 9pm. Dinner is a light hot meal, usually taken with the family.

At around 5pm, a special snack (*le goûter*) is served to children, usually a roll or slices of baguette and biscuits with some chocolate.

4.1 On arrival

I'd like to book a table for seven o'clock, please?	Puis-je réserver une table pour sept heures? *pwee jhuh rayzehrvay ewn tahbl poor seht uhr?*
I'd like a table for two, please	Une table pour deux personnes s'il vous plaît *ewn tahbl poor duh pehrson seel voo pleh*
We've/we haven't_____ booked	Nous (n')avons (pas) réservé *noo zahvawn/noo nahvawn pah rayzehrvay*
Is the restaurant open yet?	Le restaurant est déjà ouvert? *luh rehstoarohn eh dayjhah oovehr?*
What time does the restaurant open/close?	A quelle heure ouvre/ferme le restaurant? *ah kehl uhr oovr/fehrm luh rehstoarohn?*

Vous avez réservé?	Do you have a reservation?
A quel nom?	What name, please?
Par ici, s'il vous plaît.	This way, please
Cette table est réservée.	This table is reserved
Nous aurons une table de libre dans un quart d'heure.	We'll have a table free in fifteen minutes.
Voulez-vous patienter (au bar)?	Would you like to wait (at the bar)?

Can we wait for a_____ table?
Pouvons-nous attendre qu'une table soit libre?
poovawn noo zahtohndr kewn tahbl swah leebr?

Do we have to wait ____ long?
Devons-nous attendre longtemps?
devawn noo zahtohndr lawntohn?

Is this seat taken? _____
Est-ce que cette place est libre?
ehs kuh seht plahs eh leebr?

Could we sit _____ here/there?
Pouvons-nous nous asseoir ici/là-bas?
poovawn noo noo zahswahr eesee/lahbah?

Can we sit by the_____ window?
Pouvons-nous nous asseoir près de la fenêtre?
poovawn noo noo zahswahr preh duh lah fuhnehtr?

Can we eat outside? ___
Pouvons-nous aussi manger dehors?
poovawn noo zoasee mohnjhay duh-ohr?

Do you have another____ chair for us?
Avez-vous encore une chaise?
ahvay voo zohnkor ewn shehz?

Do you have a _____ highchair?
Avez-vous une chaise haute?
ahvay voo zewn shehz oat?

Is there a socket for____ this bottle-warmer?
Y a-t-il une prise pour ce chauffe-biberon?
ee ya teel ewn preez poor suh shoaf beebuhrawn?

Could you warm up _____ this bottle/jar for me?	Pouvez-vous me réchauffer ce biberon/ce petit pot?
	poovay voo muh rayshoafay suh beebuhrawn/suh puhtee poa?
Not too hot, please _____	Pas trop chaud s'il vous plaît
	pah troa shoa seel voo pleh
Is there somewhere I _____ can change the baby's nappy?	Y a-t-il ici une pièce où je peux m'occuper du bébé?
	ee ya teel eesee ewn pyehs oo jhuh puh mokewpay dew baybay?
Where are the toilets? __	Où sont les toilettes?
	oo sawn lay twahleht?

4.2 Ordering

Waiter! _____	Garçon!
	gahrsawn!
Madam! _____	Madame!
	mahdahm!
Sir!_____	Monsieur!
	muhsyuh!
We'd like something to _ eat/a drink	Nous aimerions manger/boire quelque chose
	noo zaymuhryawn mohnjhay/bwahr kehlkuh shoaz
Could I have a quick _____ meal?	Puis-je rapidement manger quelque chose?
	pwee jhuh rahpeedmohn mohnjhay kehlkuh shoaz?
We don't have much _____ time	Nous avons peu de temps
	noo zavawn puh duh tohn
We'd like to have a _____ drink first	Nous voulons d'abord boire quelque chose
	noo voolawn dahbor bwahr kehlkuh shoaz

Could we see the ___ menu/wine list, please?	Pouvons-nous avoir la carte/la carte des vins? _poovawn noo zahvwahr lah kahrt/lah kahrt day vahn?_
Do you have a menu ___ in English?	Vous avez un menu en anglais? _voo zahvay zuhn muhnew ohn nohngleh?_
Do you have a dish ___ of the day?	Vous avez un plat du jour? _voo zahvay zuhn plah dew jhoor?_
We haven't made a ___ choice yet	Nous n'avons pas encore choisi _noo nahvawn pah zohnkor shwahzee_
What do you ___ recommend?	Qu'est-ce que vous nous conseillez? _kehs kuh voo noo kawnsayay?_
What are the ___ specialities of the region/the house?	Quelles sont les spécialités de cette région/de la maison? _kehl sawn lay spaysyahleetay duh seht rayjhyawn/duh lah mehzawn?_
I like strawberries/ ___ olives	J'aime les fraises/les olives _jhehm lay frehz/lay zoleev_
I don't like meat/fish/... _	Je n'aime pas la viande/le poisson/... _jhuh nehm pah lah vyohnd/luh pwahssawn/..._
What's this? ___	Qu'est-ce que c'est? _kehs kuh seh?_

Vous désirez prendre un apéritif?	Would you like a drink first?
Vous avez déjà fait votre choix?	Have you decided?
Que désirez-vous boire?	What would you like to drink?
Bon appétit	Enjoy your meal
Vous désirez votre viande saignante, à point ou bien cuite?	Would you like your steak rare, medium or well done?
Vous désirez un dessert/du café?	Would you like a dessert/coffee?

Does it have...in it? ___	Y a-t-il du/de la/des...dedans?
	ee ya teel dew/duh lah/day...duhdohn?
What does it taste like? ___	A quoi cela ressemble-t-il?
	ah kwah suhlah ruhsohnbluh teel?
Is this a hot or a cold dish? ___	Ce plat, est-il chaud ou froid?
	suh plah, eh teel shoa oo frwah?
Is this sweet? ___	Ce plat, est-il sucré?
	suh plah, eh teel sewkray?
Is this spicy? ___	Ce plat, est-il épicé?
	suh plah, eh teel aypeesay?
Do you have anything else, please? ___	Vous avez peut-être autre chose?
	voo zahvay puh tehtr oatr shoaz?
I'm on a salt-free diet ___	Le sel m'est interdit
	luh sehl meh tahntehrdee
I can't eat pork ___	La viande de porc m'est interdite
	lah vyohnd duh por meh tahntehrdeet
– sugar ___	Le sucre m'est interdit
	luh sewkr meh tahntehrdee
– fatty foods ___	Le gras m'est interdit
	luh grah meh tahntehrdee
– (hot) spices ___	Les épices (fortes) me sont interdites
	lay zaypees (fort) muh sawn tahntehrdeet
I'll have what those people are having ___	J'aimerais la même chose que ces personnes-là
	jhehmuhreh lah mehm shoaz kuh say pehrson lah
I'd like... ___	J'aimerais...
	jhehmuhreh...
We're not having a starter ___	Nous ne prenons pas d'entrée
	noo nuh pruhnawn pah dohntray
The child will share what we're having ___	L'enfant partagera notre menu
	lohnfohn pahrtahjhuhrah notr muhnew
Could I have some more bread, please? ___	Encore du pain s'il vous plaît
	ohnkor dew pahn seel voo pleh
– a bottle of water/ wine ___	Une autre bouteille d'eau/de vin
	ewn oatr bootehy doa/duh vahn

– another helping of... _	Une autre portion de...
	ewn oatr porsyawn duh...
– some salt and _____ pepper	Pouvez-vous apporter du sel et du poivre?
	poovay voo zahportay dew sehl ay dew pwahvr?
– a napkin _____	Pouvez-vous apporter une serviette?
	poovay voo zahportay ewn sehrvyeht?
– a spoon_____	Pouvez-vous apporter une cuillère?
	poovay voo zahportay ewn kweeyehr?
– an ashtray_____	Pouvez-vous apporter un cendrier?
	poovay voo zahportay uhn sohndryay?
– some matches_____	Pouvez-vous apporter des allumettes?
	poovay voo zahportay day zahlewmeht?
– some toothpicks _____	Pouvez-vous apporter des cure-dents?
	poovay voo zahportay day kewr dohn?
– a glass of water_____	Pouvez-vous apporter un verre d'eau?
	poovay voo zahportay uhn vehr doa?
– a straw (for the child) _	Pouvez-vous apporter une paille (pour l'enfant)?
	poovay voo zahportay ewn paheey (poor lohnfohn)?
Enjoy your meal!_____	Bon appétit!
	bohn nahpaytee!
You too! _____	De même vous aussi
	duh mehm voo zoasee
Cheers!_____	Santé!
	sohntay!
The next round's on me	La prochaine tournée est pour moi
	lah proshehn toornay eh poor mwah
Could we have a _____ doggy bag, please?	Pouvons-nous emporter les restes pour notre chien?
	poovawn noo zohnportay lay rehst poor notr shyahn?

4.3 The bill

See also 8.2 Settling the bill

How much is this _____ dish?	Quel est le prix de ce plat? *kehl eh luh pree duh suh plah?*
Could I have the bill, ___ please?	L'addition s'il vous plaît *lahdeesyawn seel voo pleh*
All together _____	Tout ensemble *too tohnsohnbl*
Everyone pays _____ separately	Chacun paye pour soi *shahkuhn pehy poor swah*
Could we have the ____ menu again, please?	Pouvons-nous revoir la carte? *poovawn noo ruhvwahr lah kahrt?*
The...is not on the bill _	Le...n'est pas sur l'addition *luh...neh pah sewr lahdeesyawn*

4.4 Complaints

It's taking a very _____ long time	C'est bien long *seh byahn lawn*
We've been here an____ hour already.	Nous sommes ici depuis une heure *noo som zeesee duhpwee zewn uhr*
This must be a mistake_	Cela doit être une erreur *suhlah dwah tehtr ewn ehruhr*
This is not what I _____ ordered.	Ce n'est pas ce que j'ai commandé *suh neh pah suh kuh jhay komohnday*
I ordered..._____	J'ai commandé un... *jhay komohnday uhn...*
There's a dish missing__	Il manque un plat *eel mohnk uhn plah*
This is broken/ _____ not clean	C'est cassé/ce n'est pas propre *seh kahssay/suh neh pah propr*
The food's cold_____	Le plat est froid *luh plah eh frwah*

– not fresh _____	Le plat n'est pas frais
	luh plah neh pah freh
– too salty/sweet/spicy _	Le plat est trop salé/sucré/épicé
	luh plah eh troa sahlay/sewkray/aypeesay
The meat's not done ___	La viande n'est pas cuite
	lah vyohnd neh pah kweet
– overdone _____	La viande est trop cuite
	lah vyohnd eh troa kweet
– tough _____	La viande est dure
	lah vyohnd eh dewr
– off _____	La viande est avariée
	lah vyohnd eh tahvahryay
Could I have _____ something else instead of this?	Vous pouvez me donner autre chose à la place?
	voo poovay muh donay oatr shoaz ah lah plahs?
The bill/this amount is _ not right	L'addition/cette somme n'est pas exacte
	lahdeesyawn/seht som neh pah zehgzahkt
We didn't have this ___	Ceci nous ne l'avons pas eu
	suhsee noo nuh lahvawn pah zew
There's no paper in the _ toilet	Il n'y a plus de papier hygiénique dans les toilettes
	eel nee yah plew duh pahpyay eejhyayneek dohn lay twahleht
Do you have a _____ complaints book?	Avez-vous un registre de réclamations?
	ahvay voo zuhn ruhjheestr duh rayklahmahsyawn?
Will you call the _____ manager, please?	Voulez-vous appeler le directeur s'il vous plaît?
	voolay voo zahpuhlay luh deerehktuhr seel voo pleh?

4.5 Paying a compliment

That was a wonderful __ meal
Nous avons très bien mangé
noo zahvawn treh byahn mohnjhay

The food was excellent__
Le repas était succulent
luh ruhpah ayteh sewkewlohn

The...in particular was __ delicious
Le...surtout était délicieux
luh...sewrtoo ayteh dayleesyuh

4.6 The menu

apéritifs
aperitifs

boissons alcoolisées
alcoholic beverages

boissons chaudes
hot beverages

carte des vins
wine list

coquillages
shellfish

desserts
sweets

fromages
cheese

gibier
game

hors d'oeuvres
starters

légumes
vegetables

plats chauds
hot dishes

plats froids
cold dishes

plat du jour
dish of the day

pâtisserie
pastry

plat principal
main course

potages
soups

service compris
service included

spécialités
régionales
regional specialities

viandes
meat dishes

volailles
poultry

4.7 Alphabetical list of drinks and dishes

agneau
lamb

ail
garlic

amandes
almonds

ananas
pineapple

anchois
anchovy

anguille
eel

anis
aniseed

apéritif
aperitif

artichaut
artichoke

asperge
asparagus

baguette
french stick

banane
banana

beurre
butter

biftec
steak

bière (bière
pression)
beer (draught beer)

biscuit
biscuit

boeuf
beef

boissons alcoolisées
alcoholic beverages

boissons chaudes/
froides
hot/cold beverages

boudin noir/blanc
black/white pudding

brochet
pike

cabillaud
cod

café (noir/au lait)
coffee (black/white)

caille
quail

calmar
squid

canard
duck

câpres
capers

carpe
carp

carte des vins
wine list

céleri
celery

cerises
cherries

champignons
mushrooms

crème chantilly
cream (whipped)

châtaigne
chestnut

chausson aux
pommes
apple turnover

chou-fleur
cauliflower

choucroute
sauerkraut

chou
cabbage

choux de Bruxelles
Brussels sprouts

citron
lemon

civet de lièvre
jugged hare

clou de girofle
clove

cocktails
cocktails

cognac
brandy

concombre
cucumber

confiture
jam

consommé
broth

coquillages
shellfish

coquilles
  Saint-Jacques
scallops

cornichon
gherkin

côte/côtelette
chop

côte de boeuf
T-bone steak

côte de porc
pork chop

côtelette d'agneau
lamb chop

côtelettes dans
  l'échine
spare rib

couvert
cutlery

crabe
crab

crêpes
pancakes

crevettes grises
shrimps

crevettes roses
prawns

croissant
croissant

croque monsieur
toasted ham and
  cheese sandwich

cru
raw

crustacés
seafood

cuisses de
  grenouilles
frog's legs

cuit(à l'eau)
boiled

dattes
dates

daurade
sea bream

dessert
sweet

eau minérale
  gazeuse/non
  gazeuse
sparkling/still
  mineral water

échalote
shallot

écrevisse
crayfish

endives
chicory

entrecôte
sirloin steak

entrées
first course

épices
spices

épinards
spinach

escargots
snails

farine
flour

fenouil
fennel

fèves
broad beans

figues
figs

filet de boeuf
fillet

filet mignon
fillet steak

filet de porc
tenderloin

fines herbes
herbs

foie gras
goose liver

fraises
strawberries

framboises
raspberries

frit
fried

friture
deep-fried

fromage
cheese

fruit de la passion
passion fruit

fruits de la saison
seasonal fruits

gaufres
waffles

gigot d'agneau
leg of lamb

glace
ice cream

glaçons
ice cubes

grillé
grilled

groseilles
redcurrants

hareng
herring

haricots blancs
haricot beans

haricots verts
french beans

homard
lobster

hors d'oeuvre
starters

huîtres
oysters

jambon blanc/cru/fumé
ham(cooked/Parma style)/smoked)

jus de citron
lemon juice

jus de fruits
fruit juice

jus d'orange
orange juice

lait/demi-écrémé/ entier
milk/semi-skimmed/ full-cream

langouste
crayfish

langoustine
scampi

langue
tongue

lapin
rabbit

légumes
vegetables

lentilles
lentils

liqueur
liqueur

lotte
monkfish

loup de mer
sea bass

macaron
macaroon

maïs
sweetcorn

épis de maïs
corn (on the cob)

marron
chestnut

melon
melon

menu du jour/à la carte
menu of the day/à la carte

morilles
morels

moules
mussels

mousse au chocolat
chocolate mousse

moutarde
mustard

myrtilles
bilberries

noisette
hazelnut

noix
walnut

noix de veau
fillet of veal

oeuf à la coque/dur/au plat
egg soft/hard boiled/fried

oignon
onion

olives
olives

omelette
omelette

origan
oregano

pain au chocolat
chocolate bun

part
portion

pastis
pastis

pâtisserie
pastry

pêche
peach

petite friture
fried fish(whitebait
  or similar)

petits (biscuits)
  salés
savoury biscuits

petit pain
roll

petits pois
green peas

pigeon
pigeon

pintade
guinea fowl

plat du jour
dish of the day

plats froids/chauds
cold/hot courses

poire
pear

pois chiches
chick peas

poisson
fish

poivre
pepper

poivron
green/red pepper

pomme
apple

pommes de
  terre
potatoes

pommes frites
chips

poulet(blanc)
chicken(breast)

prune
plum

pruneaux
prunes

queue de boeuf
oxtail

ragoût
stew

ris de veau
sweetbread

riz
rice

rôti de boeuf
  (rosbif)
roast beef

rouget
red mullet

saignant
rare

salade verte
lettuce

salé/sucré
salted/sweet

sandwich
sandwich

saumon
salmon

sel
salt

service compris/non
  compris
service (not) included

sole
sole

soupe
soup

soupe à l'oignon
onion soup

spécialités
  régionales
regional specialities

sucre
sugar

thon
tuna

thym
thyme

tripes
tripe

truffes
truffles

truite
trout

truite saumonée
salmon trout

turbot
turbot

vapeur (à la)
steamed

venaison
venison

viande hachée
minced meat/mince

vin blanc
white wine

vin rosé	vinaigre
rosé wine	vinegar
vin rouge	xérès
red wine	sherry

5 On the road

5.1 Asking for directions

Excuse me, could I ask you something?	Pardon, puis-je vous demander quelque chose? *pahrdawn, pwee jhuh voo duhmohnday kehlkuh shoaz?*
I've lost my way _____	Je me suis égaré(e) *jhuh muh swee zaygahray*
Is there an... around here?	Connaissez-vous un...dans les environs? *konehssay voo zuhn... dohn lay zohnveerawn?*
Is this the way to...? ___	Est-ce la route vers...? *ehs lah root vehr...?*
Could you tell me how to get to...?	Pouvez-vous me dire comment aller à...? *poovay voo muh deer komohn tahlay ah...?*
What's the quickest way to...?	Comment puis-je arriver le plus vite possible à...? *komohn pwee jhuh ahreevay luh plew veet pohseebl ah...?*
How many kilometres is it to...?	Il y a encore combien de kilomètres jusqu'à...? *eel ee yah ohnkor kohnbyahn duh keeloamehtr jhewskah...?*

Je ne sais pas, je ne suis pas d'ici	I don't know, I don't know my way around here
Vous vous êtes trompé	You're going the wrong way
Vous devez retourner à... Là-bas les panneaux vous indiqueront la route	You have to go back to... From there on just follow the signs
Là-bas vous demanderez à nouveau votre route	When you get there, ask again

Could you point it _____ out on the map?

Pouvez-vous me l'indiquer sur la carte?
poovay voo muh lahndeekay sewr lah kahrt?

tout droit straight ahead	le feu (de signalisation) the traffic light	le pont the bridge
à gauche left	le tunnel the tunnel	le passage à niveau the level crossing
à droite right	le panneau `cédez la priorité' the `give way' sign	la barrière boom
tourner turn	l'immeuble the building	le panneau direction... the sign pointing to...
suivre follow	à l'angle, au coin at the corner	la flèche the arrow
traverser cross	la rivière, le fleuve the river	
le carrefour the intersection	l'autopont the fly-over	
la rue the street		

5.2 Customs

● **Border documents** along with your passport you must carry your original documents with you. These include your valid full driving licence (together with paper counterpart if photocard licence), vehicle registration document and motor insurance certificate. Contact your motor insurer for advice at least a month before taking your vehicle overseas to ensure that you are adequately covered. It is advisable to carry a fire extinguisher, first-aid kit and warning triangle. Entry regulations can change at very short notice, so you are advised to check with your travel agent, airline, ferry or rail company that you have the correct documentation before your journey.

Votre passeport s'il vous plaît	Your passport, please
La carte verte s'il vous plaît	Your green card, please
La carte grise s'il vous plaît	Your vehicle documents, please
Votre visa s'il vous plaît	Your visa, please
Où allez-vous?	Where are you heading?
Combien de temps pensez-vous rester?	How long are you planning to stay?
Avez-vous quelque chose à déclarer?	Do you have anything to declare?
Voulez-vous l'ouvrir?	Open this, please

My children are _____ entered on this passport	Mes enfants sont inscrits dans ce passeport
	may zohnfohn sawn tahnskree dohn suh pahspor
I'm travelling through___	Je suis de passage
	jhuh swee duh pahsahjh
I'm going on holiday ___ to...	Je vais en vacances en...
	jhuh veh zohn vahkohns ohn...
I'm on a business trip __	Je suis en voyage d'affaires
	jhuh swee zohn vwahyahjh dahfehr
I don't know how _____ long I'll be staying yet	Je ne sais pas encore combien de temps je reste
	jhuh nuh seh pah zohnkor kawnbyahn duh tohn jhuh rehst
I'll be staying here for __ a weekend	Je reste un week-end ici
	jhuh rehst uhn weekehnd eesee
– for a few days _____	Je reste quelques jours ici
	jhuh rehst kehlkuh jhoor eesee
– for a week _____	Je reste une semaine ici
	jhuh rehst ewn suhmehn eesee
–for two weeks _____	Je reste quinze jours ici
	jhuh rehst kahnz jhoor eesee

I've got nothing to declare	Je n'ai rien à déclarer *jhuh nay ryahn nah dayklahray*
I've got...with me	J'ai... avec moi *jhay... ahvehk mwah*
– ...cartons of cigarettes	J'ai des cartouches de cigarettes *jhay day kahrtoosh duh seegahreht*
– ...bottles of...	J'ai des bouteilles de... *jhay day bootehy duh...*
– some souvenirs	J'ai quelques souvenirs *jhay kehlkuh soovneer*
These are personal effects	Ce sont des affaires personnelles *suh sawn day zahfehr pehrsonehl*
These are not new	Ces affaires ne sont pas neuves *say zahfehr nuh sawn pah nuhv*
Here's the receipt	Voici la facture *vwahsee lah fahktewr*
This is for private use	C'est pour usage personnel *seh poor ewzahjh pehrsonehl*
How much import duty do I have to pay?	Combien de droits d'importation dois-je payer? *kawnbyahn duh drwah dahnpohrtasyawn dwah jhuh payay?*
Can I go now?	Puis-je partir maintenant? *pwee jhuh pahrteer mahntuhnohn?*

5.3 Luggage

Porter!	Porteur! *portuhr!*
Could you take this luggage to...?	Voulez-vous porter ces bagages à... s'il vous plaît? *voolay voo portay say bahgahjh ah... seel voo pleh?*
How much do I owe you?	Combien vous dois-je? *kawnbyahn voo dwah jhuh?*

Where can I find a _____ luggage trolley?	Où puis-je trouver un chariot pour les bagages?
	oo pwee jhuh troovay uhn shahryoa poor lay bahgahjh?
Could you store this _____ luggage for me?	Puis-je mettre ces bagages en consigne?
	pwee jhuh mehtr say bahgahjh ohn kawnseenyuh?
Where are the luggage _ lockers?	Où est la consigne automatique?
	oo eh lah kawnseenyuh oatoamahteek?
I can't get the locker _____ open	Je n'arrive pas à ouvrir la consigne
	jhuh nahreev pah zah oovreer lah kawnseenyuh
How much is it _____ per item per day?	Combien cela coûte-t-il par bagage par jour?
	kawnbyahn suhlah koot-uh teel pahr bahgahjh pahr jhoor?
This is not my bag/ _____ suitcase	Ce n'est pas mon sac/ma valise
	suh neh pah mawn sahk/mah vahleez
There's one item/bag/ __ suitcase missing still	Il manque encore une chose/un sac/une valise
	eel mohnk ohnkor ewn shoaz/uhn sahk/ewn vahleez
My suitcase is_____ damaged	Ma valise est abîmée
	mah vahleez eh tahbeemay

5.4 Traffic signs

| accès interdit à tous les véhicules no entry | allumez vos feux switch on lights | bison fûté recommended route |
| accotement non stabilisé soft verge | autoroute motorway barrière de dégel road closed | brouillard fréquent beware fog cédez le passage give way |

chaussée à gravillons
loose chippings

chaussée déformée
uneven road surface

chaussée glissante
slippery road

circulation alternée
alternate priority

danger
danger

carrefour dangereux
dangerous crossing

danger priorité à droite
priority to vehicles from right

descente dangereuse
steep hill

déviation
diversion

fin de...
end of...

fin d'allumage des feux
end of need for lights

fin de chantier
end of road works

interdiction de dépasser
no overtaking

interdiction de klaxonner
no horns

interdiction sauf riverains
access only

limite de vitesse
speed limit

passage à niveau
level crossing

passage d'animaux
animals crossing

passage pour piétons
pedestrian crossing

péage
toll

poids lourds
heavy goods vehicles

rappel
reminder

remorques et semi-remorques
lorries and articulated lorries

sens unique
one-way traffic

serrez à droite
keep right

sortie
exit

sortie de camions
factory/works exit

interdiction de stationner
no parking

taxis
taxi rank

travaux (sur...km)
roadworks ahead

véhicules lents
slow traffic

véhicules transportant des matières dangereuses
vehicles transporting dangerous substances

verglas fréquent
ice on road

virages sur...km
bends for...km

vitesse limite
maximum speed

zone bleue
parking disc required

zone piétonne
pedestrian zone

5.5 The car

● Particular traffic regulations:
–maximum speed for cars:
130km/h on toll roads, 110km/h in wet weather
110km/h on other motorways, 100km/h in wet weather
90km/h outside built-up areas, 80km/h in wet weather
50km/h in built-up areas
It is recommended that all vehicles used dipped headlights day and night outside built-up areas.

5.6 The petrol station

● **Petrol is equally expensive** in France although diesel can be cheaper.

How many kilometres __ to the next petrol station, please?	Il y a combien de kilomètres jusqu'à la prochaine station-service?
	eel ee yah kawnbyahn duh keeloamehtr jhewskah lah proshehn stasyawn sehrvees?
I would like...litres of..., _ please	Je voudrais ... litres
	jhuh voodreh ... leetr
– 4-star_____	Je voudrais ... litres de super
	jhuh voodreh ... leetr duh sewpehr
– leaded_____	Je voudrais ... litres d'essence ordinaire
	jhuh voodreh ... leetr dehssohns ohrdeenehr
– unleaded_____	Je voudrais ... litres d'essence sans plomb
	jhuh voodreh ... leetr dehssohns sohn plawn

– diesel_____	Je voudrais ... litres de gazoil
	jhuh voodreh ... leetr duh gahzwahl
I would like...euros_____	Je voudrais pour ... euros d'essence s'il
worth of petrol, please.	vous plaît
	jhuh voodreh poor ... frohn dehssohns seel
	voo pleh
Fill it up, please _____	Le plein s'il vous plaît
	luh plahn seel voo pleh
Could you check...?____	Vous voulez contrôler...?
	voo voolay kawntroalay...?
– the oil level_____	Vous voulez contrôler le niveau d'huile?
	voo voolay kawntroalay luh neevoa dweel?
– the tyre pressure_____	Vous voulez contrôler la pression des
	pneus?
	voo voolay kawntroalay lah prehsyawn day
	pnuh?
Could you change the___	Vous pouvez changer l'huile?
oil, please?	*voo poovay shohnjhay lweel?*
Could you clean the ___	Vous pouvez nettoyer les vitres/le
windows/the	pare-brise?
windscreen, please?	*voo poovay nehtwahyay lay veetr/luh*
	pahrbreez?
Could you give the car _	Vous pouvez faire laver la voiture?
a wash, please?	*voo poovay fehr lahvay lah vwahtewr?*

The parts of a car

battery	la batterie	*lah bahtree*
rear light	le feu arrière	*luh fuh ahryehr*
rear-view mirror	le rétroviseur	*luh raytroaveezuhr*
reversing light	le phare de recul	*luh fahr duh ruhkewl*
aerial	l'antenne(f.)	*lohntehn*
car radio	l'autoradio(m.)	*loatoarahdyoa*
petrol tank	le réservoir d'essence	*luh rayzehrvwahr dehssohns*
inside mirror	le rétroviseur intérieur	*luh raytroaveezuhr ahntayryuhr*
sparking plugs	les bougies(f.)	*llay boojhee*
fuel filter/pump	le filtre à carburant la pompe à carburant	*luh feeltr ah kahrbewrohn lah pawnp ah kahrbewrohn*
wing mirror	le rétroviseur de côté	*luh raytroaveezuhr duh koatay*
bumper	le pare-chocs	*luh pahr shok*
carburettor	le carburateur	*luh kahrbewrahtuhr*
crankcase	le carter	*lluh kahrtehr*
cylinder	le cylindre	*luh seelahndr*
ignition	l'allumage	*l'ahlewmahjh*
warning light	la lampe témoin	*lah lohnp taymwahn*
dynamo	la dynamo	*lah deenahmoa*
accelerator	l'accélérateur	*lahksaylayrahtuhr*
handbrake	le frein à main	*luh frahn ah mahn*
valve	la soupape	*lah soopahp*
silencer	le silencieux	*luh seelohnsyuh*
boot	le coffre	*luh kofr*
headlight	le phare	*luh fahr*
crank shaft	le vilebrequin	*luh veelbruhkahn*
air filter	le filtre à air	*luh feeltr ah ehr*
fog lamp	le phare anti-brouillar	*luh fahr ohntee brooy-yahr*

engine block	le bloc moteur	luh blok motuhr
camshaft	l'arbre à cames	lahrbr ah kahm
oil filter/pump	le filtre à huile	luh feeltr ah weel
	la pompe à huile	lah pawnp ah weel
dipstick	la jauge du niveau d'huile	lah jhoajh dew neevoa dweel
pedal	la pédale	lah paydahl
door	la portière	lah portyehr
radiator	le radiateur	luh rahdyahtuhr
disc brake	le frein à disque	luh frahn ah deesk
spare wheel	la roue de secours	lah roo duh suhkoor
indicator	le clignotant	luh kleenyohtohn
windscreen wiper	l'essuie-glace(m.)	lehswee glahs
shock absorbers	les amortisseurs(m.)	lay zahmorteesuhr
sunroof	le toit ouvrant	luh twah oovrohn
starter motor	le démarreur	luh daymahruhr
steering column	la colonne de direction	lah kolon duh deerehksyawn
steering wheel	le volant	luh volohn
exhaust pipe	le tuyau d'échappement	luh tweeyoa dayshahpmohn
seat belt	la ceinture de sécurité	lah sahntewr duh saykewreetay
fan	le ventilateur	luh vohnteelahtuhr
distributor cable	le câble distributeur	luh kahbl deestreebewtuhr
gear lever	le levier de vitesses	luh luhvyay duh veetehs
windscreen	le pare-brise	luh pahrbreez
water pump	la pompe à eau	lah pawnp ah oa
wheel	la roue	lah roo
hubcap	l'enjoliveur	lohnjholeevuhr
piston	le piston	luh peestawn

73

The parts of a bicycle

rear lamp	le feu arrière	luh fuh ahryehr
rear wheel	la roue arrière	lah roo ahryehr
(luggage) carrier	le porte-bagages	luh port bahgahjh
bicycle fork	la tête de fourche	lah teht duh foorsh
bell	la sonnette	lah sohneht
inner tube	la chambre à air	lah shohnbr ah ehr
tyre	le pneu	luh pnuh
crank	le pédalier	luh paydahlyay
gear change	le changement de vitesse	luh shohnjhmohn duh veetehs
wire	le fil (électrique)	luh feel (aylehktreek)
dynamo	la dynamo	lah deenahmoa
bicycle trailer	la remorque de bicyclette	lah ruhmork duh beeseekleht
frame	le cadre	luh kahdr
dress guard	le protège-jupe	luh protehjh jhewp
chain	la chaîne	lah shehn
chainguard	le carter	luh kahrtehr
padlock	l'antivol(m.)	lohnteevol
milometer	le compteur kilométrique	luh kawntuhr keeloamaytreek
child's seat	le siège-enfant	luh syehjh ohnfohn
headlamp	le phare	luh fahr
bulb	l'ampoule(f.)	lohnpool
pedal	la pédale	lah paydahl
pump	la pompe	lah pawnp
reflector	le réflecteur	luh rayflehktuhr
break blocks	les patins	lay pahtahn
brake cable	le câble de frein	luh kahbl duh frahn
wheel lock	le cadenas pour bicyclette	lah kaduhnah poor beeseekleht
carrier straps	le tendeur	luh tohnduhr

tachometer	le compteur de vitesse	*luh kawntuhr duh veetehs*
spoke	le rayon	*luh rayawn*
mudguard	le garde-boue	*luh gahrd boo*
handlebar	le guidon	*luh gueedawn*
chain wheel	le pignon	*luh peenyawn*
toe clip	le câle-pied	*luh kahl pyay*
crank axle	l'axe du pédalier(m.)	*lahx dew paydahlyay*
drum brake	le frein à tambour	*luh frahn ah tohnboor*
rim	la jante	*lah jhohnt*
valve	la valve	*lah vahlv*
valve tube	le raccord souple de la valve	*luh rahkor soopl duh lah vahlv*
gear cable	la chaîne du dérailleur	*lah shehn dew dayrahyuhr*
fork	la fourche	*lah foorsh*
front wheel	la roue avant	*lah roo ahvohn*
saddle	la selle	*lah sehl*

5.7 Breakdown and repairs

I'm having car trouble. Could you give me a hand?	Je suis en panne. Vous pouvez m'aider? _jhuh swee zohn pahnn. voo poovay mayday?_
I've run out of petrol	Je n'ai plus d'essence _jhuh neh plew dehssohns_
I've locked the keys in the car	J'ai laissé les clefs dans la voiture fermée _jhay layssay lay klay dohn lah vwahtewr fehrmay_
The car/motorbike/ moped won't start	La voiture/la moto/le vélomoteur ne démarre pas _lah vwahtewr/lah moatoa/luh vayloamotuhr nuh daymahr pah_
Could you contact the recovery service for me, please?	Vous pouvez m'appeler l'assistance routière? _voo poovay mahpuhlay lahseestohns rootyehr?_
Could you call a garage for me,please?	Vous pouvez m'appeler un garage? _voo poovay mahpuhlay uhn gahrahjh?_
Could you give me a lift to...?	Puis-je aller avec vous jusqu'à ...? _pwee jhahlay ahvehk voo jhewskah ...?_
– a garage/into town?	Puis-je aller avec vous jusqu'à un garage/la ville? _pwee jhahlay ahvehk voo jhewskah uhn gahrahjh/lah veel?_
– a phone booth?	Puis-je aller avec vous jusqu'à une cabine téléphonique? _pwee jhahlay ahvehk voo jhewskah ewn kahbeen taylayfoneek?_
– an emergency phone?	Puis-je aller avec vous jusqu'à un téléphone d'urgence? _pwee jhalay ahvehk voo jhewskah uhn taylayfon dewrjhohns?_

Can we take my _____ bicycle/moped?	Est-ce que vous pouvez également prendre mon vélo(moteur)?	*ehs kuh voo poovay aygahlmohn prohndr mawn vayloa(motuhr)?*
Could you tow me to___ a garage?	Vous pouvez me remorquer jusqu'à un garage?	*voo poovay muh ruhmorkay jhewskah uhn gahrahjh?*
There's probably_____ something wrong with...(See page 50)	Le ... a certainement quelque chose de défectueux	*luh ... ah sehrtehnemohn kehlkuh shoaz duh dayfehktewuh*
Can you fix it? _____	Vous pouvez le réparer?	*voo poovay luh raypahray?*
Could you fix my tyre? _	Vous pouvez réparer mon pneu?	*voo poovay raypahray mawn pnuh?*
Could you change this _ wheel?	Vous pouvez changer cette roue?	*voo poovay shohnjhay seht roo?*
Can you fix it so it'll____ get me to...?	Vous pouvez le réparer pour que je puisse rouler jusqu'à...?	*voo poovay luh raypahray poor kuh jhuh pwees roolay jhewskah...?*
Which garage can _____ help me?	Quel garage pourrait m'aider?	*kehl gahrahjh pooreh mayday?*
When will my_____ car/bicycle be ready?	Quand est-ce que ma voiture/ma bicyclette sera prête?	*kohn tehs kuh mah vwahtewr/mah beeseekleht suhrah preht?*
Can I wait for it here? __	Je peux l'attendre ici?	*jhuh puh lahtohndr eesee?*
How much will it cost? _	Combien cela va coûter?	*kawnbyahn suhlah vah kootay?*
Could you itemise _____ the bill?	Vous pouvez me détailler la note?	*voo poovay muh daytahyay lah not?*

| Can I have a receipt for the insurance? | Puis-je avoir un reçu pour l'assurance? *pwee jhahvwahr uhn ruhsew poor lahsewrohns?* |

5.8 The bicycle/moped

● **Cycle paths** are rare in France. Bikes can be hired at tourist centres (*vélo tout terrain* = mountain bike). Not much consideration for bikes should be expected on the roads. The maximum speed for mopeds is 45km/h both inside and outside town centres. A helmet is compulsory.

Je n'ai pas les pièces détachées pour votre voiture/bicyclette	I don't have parts for your car/bicycle
Je dois aller chercher les pièces détachées ailleurs	I have to get the parts from somewhere else
Je dois commander les pièces détachées	I have to order the parts
Cela prendra une demi-journée	That'll take half a day
Cela prendra une journée	That'll take a day
Cela prendra quelques jours	That'll take a few days
Cela prendra une semaine	That'll take a week
Votre voiture est bonne pour la ferraille	Your car is a write-off
Il n'y a plus rien à y faire	It can't be repaired.
La voiture/la moto/la mobylette/la bicyclette sera prête à... heures	The car/motor bike/moped/bicycle will be ready at... o'clock.

5.9 Renting a vehicle

I'd like to rent a... _____	J'aimerais louer un...
	jhehmuhreh looay uhn...
Do I need a (special) ___ licence for that?	Me faut-il un permis spécial?
	muh foa teel uhn pehrmee spaysyal?
I'd like to rent the... ___ for...	Je voudrais louer le/la...pour
	jhuh voodreh looay luh/lah...poor
– one day_____	Je voudrais louer le/la...pour une journée
	jhuh voodreh looay luh/lah...poor ewn jhoornay
– two days _____	Je voudrais louer le/la...pour deux jours
	jhuh voodreh looay luh/lah...poor duh jhoor
How much is that per ___ day/week?	C'est combien par jour/semaine?
	seh kawnbyahn pahr jhoor/suhmehn?
How much is the _____ deposit?	De combien est la caution?
	duh kawnbyahn eh lah koasyawn?
Could I have a receipt___ for the deposit?	Puis-je avoir un reçu pour la caution?
	pwee jhahvwahr uhn ruhsew poor lah koasyawn?
How much is the _____ surcharge per kilometre?	Quel est le supplément par kilomètre?
	kehl eh luh sewplaymohn pahr keeloamehtr?
Does that include_____ petrol?	Est-ce que l'essence est incluse?
	ehs kuh lehsohns eh tahnklewz?
Does that include_____ insurance?	Est-ce que l'assurance est incluse?
	ehs kuh lahsewrohns eh tahnklewz?
What time can I pick ___ the...up tomorrow?	Demain, à quelle heure puis-je venir chercher la...?
	duhmahn ah kehl uhr pwee jhuh vuhneer shehrshay lah...?
When does the...have __ to be back?	Quand dois-je rapporter la...?
	kohn dwah jhuh rahportay lah...?

Where's the petrol tank?	Où est le réservoir?
	oo eh luh rayzehrvwahr?
What sort of fuel does it take?	Quel carburant faut-il utiliser?
	kehl kahrbewrohn foa teel ewteeleezay?

5.10 Hitchhiking

Where are you heading?	Où allez-vous?
	oo ahlay voo?
Can I come along?	Pouvez-vous m'emmener en voiture?
	poovay voo momuhnay ohn vwahtewr?
Can my boyfriend/ girlfriend come too?	Mon ami(e), peut-il/peut-elle venir avec nous?
	mawn nahmee, puh teel/puh tehl vuhneer ahvehk noo?
I'm trying to get to...	Je dois aller à...
	jhuh dwah zahlay ah...
Is that on the way to...?	C'est sur la route de...?
	seh sewr lah root duh...?
Could you drop me off...?	Vous pouvez me déposer...?
	voo poovay muh daypoazay...?
– here?	Vous pouvez me déposer ici?
	voo poovay muh daypoazay eesee?
– at the...exit?	Vous pouvez me déposer à la sortie vers...?
	voo poovay muh daypoazay ah lah sohrtee vehr...?
– in the centre?	Vous pouvez me déposer dans le centre?
	voo poovay muh daypoazay dohn luh sohntr?
– at the next roundabout?	Vous pouvez me déposer au prochain rond-point?
	voo poovay muh daypoazay oa proshahn rawnpwahn?

Could you stop here, please?	**Voulez-vous arrêter ici s'il vous plaît?**
	voolay voo zahrehtay eesee seel voo pleh?
I'd like to get out here	**Je voudrais descendre ici**
	jhuh voodreh duhsohndr eesee
Thanks for the lift	**Merci pour la route**
	mehrsee poor lah root

6.1 In general

● **You can check** departure times by telephone or minitel – a computerised information system widely available in France (for example in many post offices). Tickets for buses and the *métro* (Paris, Lyon and Marseille) are cheaper when bought in a *carnet* (book of ten), available at kiosks near some bus stops, at newsagents and in *métro* stations.

Announcements

Le train de...heures, en direction de... a un retard de... minutes.	The...train to...has been delayed by...minutes
Le train en direction de.../en provenance de...arrive sur le quai...	The train now arriving at platform...is the...train to .../from...
Le train en direction de...va quitter le quai...dans quelques instants.	The train to...is about to leave from platform...
Attention éloignez-vous de la voie, un train rapide va passer sur la voie...	Attention please, keep your distance from the rail track, an intercity train will pass on platform...
Nous approchons la gare de...	We're now approaching...

Where does this train go to?	Où va ce train? *oo vah suh trahn?*
Does this boat go to...?	Ce bateau, va-t-il à...? *suh bahtoa, vah teel ah...?*
Can I take this bus to...?	Puis-je prendre ce bus pour aller à...? *pwee jhuh prondr suh bews poor ahlay ah...?*

Does this train stop at...?	Ce train s'arrête-t-il à...?
	suh trahn sahreht-uh-teel ah...?
Is this seat taken/free/reserved?	Est-ce que cette place est occupée/libre/réservée?
	ehs kuh seht plahs eh tokewpay/leebr/rayzehrvay?
I've booked...	J'ai réservé...
	jhay rayzehrvay...
Could you tell me where I have to get off for... ?	Voulez-vous me dire où descendre pour...?
	voolay voo muh deer oo duhsohndr poor...?
Could you let me know when we get to...?	Voulez-me prévenir lorsque nous serons à...?
	voolay voo muh prayvuhneer lorskuh noo suhrawn zah...?
Could you stop at the next stop, please?	Voulez-vous vous arrêter au prochain arrêt s'il vous plaît?
	voolay voo voo zahrehtay oa proshahn nahreht seel voo pleh?
Where are we now?	Où sommes-nous ici?
	oo som noo zeesee?
Do I have to get off here?	Dois-je descendre ici?
	dwah jhuh duhsohndr eesee?
Have we already passed...?	Avons-nous déjà dépassé...?
	ahvawn noo dayjhah daypahsay...?
How long have I been asleep?	Combien de temps ai-je dormi?
	kawnbyahn duh tohn ay jhuh dormee?
How long does... stop here?	Combien de temps...reste ici?
	kawnbyahn duh tohn...rehst eesee?
Can I come back on the same ticket?	Puis-je revenir avec ce billet?
	pwee jhuh ruhvuhneer ahvehk suh beeyeh?
Can I change on this ticket?	Puis-je prendre une correspondance avec ce billet?
	pwee jhuh prondr ewn korehspawndohns ahvehk suh beeyeh?

How long is this ticket__ valid for?	Combien de temps ce billet reste-t-il valable?
	kawnbyahn duh tohn suh beeyeh rehst-uh-teel vahlahbl?
How much is the _____ supplement for the TGV (high speed train)?	Combien coûte le supplément pour le TGV?
	kawnbyahn koot luh sewplaymohn poor luh tayjhayvay?

6.2 Questions to passengers

Ticket types

Première classe ou deuxième classe?	First or second class?
Aller simple ou retour?	Single or return?
Fumeurs ou non fumeurs?	Smoking or non-smoking?
Côté fenêtre ou côté couloir?	Window or aisle?
A l'avant ou à l'arrière?	Front or back?
Place assise ou couchette?	Seat or couchette?
Au-dessus, au milieu ou au-dessous?	Top, middle or bottom?
Classe touriste ou classe affaires?	Tourist class or business class?
Une cabine ou un fauteuil?	Cabin or seat?
Une personne ou deux personnes?	Single or double?
Vous êtes combien de personnes à voyager?	How many are travelling?

Destination

Où allez-vous?	Where are you travelling?
Quand partez-vous?	When are you leaving?
Votre...part à...	Your...leaves at...
Vous devez prendre une correspondance	You have to change trains
Vous devez descendre à...	You have to get off at...
Vous devez passer par...	You have to travel via...
L'aller est le..	The outward journey is on...
Le retour est le...	The return journey is on...
Vous devez être à bord au plus tard à...	You have to be on board by...

On board

Votre billet s'il vous plaît	Your ticket, please
Votre réservation s'il vous plaît	Your reservation, please
Votre passeport s'il vous plaît	Your passport, please
Vous n'êtes pas à la bonne place	You're in the wrong seat
Vous êtes dans le mauvais...	You're on/in the wrong...
Cette place est réservée	This seat is reserved
Vous devez payer un supplément	You'll have to pay a supplement
Le...a un retard de...minutes	The...has been delayed by...minutes

6.3 Tickets

Where can I...? _____	Où puis-je...?
	oo pwee jhuh...?
– buy a ticket? _____	Où puis-je acheter un billet?
	oo pwee jhahshtay uhn beeyeh?
– make a reservation? __	Où puis-je réserver une place?
	oo pwee jhuh rayzehrvay ewn plahs?
– book a flight? _____	Où puis-je réserver un vol?
	oo pwee jhuh rayzehrvay uhn vol?
Could I have a...to..., _____ please?	Puis-je avoir...en direction de...?
	pwee jhahvwahr...ohn deerehksyawn duh...?
– a single _____	Puis-je avoir un aller simple?
	pwee jhahvwahr uhn nahlay sahnpl?
– a return _____	Puis-je avoir un aller-retour?
	pwee jhahvwahr uhn nahlay ruhtoor?
first class _____	première classe
	pruhmyehr klahs
second class _____	deuxième classe
	duhzyehm klahs
tourist class _____	classe touriste
	klahs tooreest
business class _____	classe affaires
	klahs ahfehr
I'd like to book a _____ seat/couchette/cabin	Je voudrais réserver une place assise/couchette/cabine
	jhuh voodreh rayzehrvay ewn plahs ahseez/koosheht/kahbeen
I'd like to book a berth _ in the sleeping car	Je voudrais réserver une place dans le wagon-lit
	jhuh voodreh rayzehrvay ewn plahs dohn luh vahgawnlee
top/middle/bottom _____	au-dessus/au milieu/au-dessous
	oaduhsew/ oa meelyuh/ oa duhsoo

smoking/no smoking ___	**fumeurs/non fumeurs**
	fewmuhr/ nawn fewmuhr
by the window _____	**à côté de la fenêtre**
	ah koatay duh lah fenehtr
single/double _____	**une personne/deux personnes**
	ewn pehrson/duh pehrson
at the front/back_____	**à l'avant/à l'arrière**
	ah lahvohn/ah lahryehr
There are...of us _____	**Nous sommes...personnes**
	noo som...pehrson
a car _____	**une voiture**
	ewn vwahtewr
a caravan_____	**une caravane**
	ewn kahrahvahnn
...bicycles_____	**...bicyclettes**
	...beeseekleht
Do you also have...? ___	**Avez-vous aussi...?**
	ahvay voo zoasee...?
– season tickets? _____	**Avez-vous aussi une carte d'abonnement?**
	ahvay voo zoasee ewn kahrt dahbonmohn?
– weekly tickets? _____	**Avez-vous aussi une carte hebdomadaire?**
	ahvay voo zoasee ewn kahrt ehbdomahdehr?
– monthly season_____ tickets?	**Avez-vous aussi une carte mensuelle?**
	ahvay voo zoasee ewn kahrt mohnsewehl?

6.4 Information

Where's? _____	**Où se trouve...?**
	oo suh troov...?

Where's the _____ information desk?	Où se trouve le bureau de renseignements?
	oo suh troov luh bewroa duh rohnsehnyuhmohn?
Where can I find a _____ timetable?	Où se trouvent les horaires des départs/des arrivées?
	oo se troov lay zorehr day daypahr/day zahreevay?
Where's the...desk? _____	Où se trouve la réception de...?
	oo se troov lah raysehpsyawn duh...?
Do you have a city _____ map with the bus/the underground routes on it?	Avez-vous un plan du réseau des bus/du métro?
	ahvay voo zuhn plohn dew rayzoa day bews/dew maytroa?
Do you have a _____ timetable?	Avez-vous un horaire des arrivées et des départs?
	ahvay voo zuhn norehr day zahreevay ay day daypahr?
I'd like to confirm/ _____ cancel/change my booking for...	Je veux confirmer/annuler/changer ma réservation pour...
	jhuh vuh kawnfeermay/ahnewlay/shohnjhay mah rayzehrvahsyawn poor...
Will I get my money_____ back?	Mon argent me sera rendu?
	mawn nahrjhohn muh suhrah rohndew?
I want to go to..._____ How do I get there? (What's the quickest way there?)	Je dois aller à...Comment puis-je y aller (le plus vite possible)?
	jhuh dwah zahlay ah...komohn pwee jhee ahlay (luh plew veet poseebl?)
How much is a _____ single/return to...?	Combien coûte un aller simple/un aller-retour pour...?
	kawnbyahn koot uhn nahlay sahnpl/uhn nahlay retoor poor...?
Do I have to pay a _____ supplement?	Dois-je payer un supplément?
	dwah jheuh payay uhn sewplaymohn?

Can I interrupt my _____ journey with this ticket?
Puis-je interrompre mon voyage avec ce billet?
pwee jhahntayrawnpr mawn vwahyahjh ahvehk suh beeyeh?

How much luggage _____ am I allowed?
J'ai droit à combien de bagages?
jhay drwah ah kawnbyahn duh bahgahjh?

Does this...travel _____ direct?
Ce...est direct?
suh...eh deerehkt?

Do I have to change? _____ Where?
Dois-je changer? Où?
dwah jhuh shohnjhay? oo?

Will this plane make _____ any stopovers?
L'avion fait escale?
lahvyawn feh tehskahl?

Does the boat call in at_ any ports on the way?
Est-ce que le bateau fait escale dans un port pendant son trajet?
ehs kuh luh bahtoa feh tehskahl dohn zuhn por pohndohn sawn trahjheh?

Does the train/ _____ bus stop at...?
Est-ce que le train/le bus s'arrête à...?
ehs kuh luh trahn/luh bews sahreht ah...?

Where should I get off?_ Où dois-je descendre?
oo dwah jhuh duhsohndr?

Is there a connection_____ to...?
Y a-t-il une correspondance pour...?
ee yah teel ewn korehspawndohns poor...?

How long do I have to__ wait?
Combien de temps dois-je attendre?
kawnbyahn duh tohn dwah jhahtohndr?

When does...leave? _____ Quand part...? *kohn pahr...?*

What time does the _____ first/next/last...leave?
A quelle heure part le premier/prochain/dernier...?
ah kehl uhr pahr luh pruhmyay/proshahn/dehrnyay...?

How long does...take? _ Combien de temps met le...?
kawnbyahn duh tohn meh luh...?

What time does...arrive_ in...?
A quelle heure arrive...à...?
ah kehl uhr ahreev...ah...?

Where does the...to... __ leave from?
D'où part le...pour...?
doo pahr luh...poor...?

Is this...to...? _____ Est-ce le...pour...?
ehs luh...poor...?

6.5 Aeroplanes

● **At arrival** at a French airport (*aéroport*), you will find the following signs:

arrivée	départ
arrivals	departures

6.6 Trains

● **The rail network** is extensive. *La Société Nationale des Chemins de Fer Français (SNCF)* is responsible for the national rail traffic. Besides the normal train, there is also *le Train à Grande Vitesse (TGV)* for which you will have to pay a supplement. Reservations before departure are cheaper. The TGV operates between the larger cities: Paris, Lyon, Marseille and Nice. A train ticket has to be stamped (*composté*) before departure.

6.7 Taxis

● **In nearly all** large cities, there are plenty of taxis. French taxis have no fixed colour. Virtually all taxis have a meter. In the smaller towns, it is usual to agree a fixed price in advance. A supplement is usual for luggage, a journey at night, on a Sunday or Bank holiday, or to an airport. It is advisable in large cities such as Paris and Lyon to check that the meter has been returned to zero at the start of the journey.

libre	occupé	station de taxis
for hire	booked	taxi rank

Taxi!	**Taxi!** *tahksee!*
Could you get me a taxi, please?	**Pouvez-vous m'appeler un taxi?** *poovay voo mahpuhlay uhn tahksee?*
Where can I find a taxi around here?	**Où puis-je prendre un taxi par ici?** *oo pwee jhuh prohndr uhn tahksee pahr eesee?*
Could you take me to..., please?	**Conduisez-moi à...s'il vous plaît.** *kawndweezay mwah ah...seel voo pleh*
– this address	**Conduisez-moi à cette adresse.** *kawndweezay mwah ah seht ahdrehs*
– the...hotel	**Conduisez-moi à l'hôtel...** *kawndweezay mwah ah loatehl...*
– the town/city centre	**Conduisez-moi dans le centre.** *kawndweezay mwah dohn luh sohntr*
– the station	**Conduisez-moi à la gare.** *kawndweezay mwah ah lah gahr*
– the airport	**Conduisez-moi à l'aéroport.** *kawndweezay mwah ah layroapor.*
How much is the trip to...?	**Combien coûte un trajet jusqu'à...?** *kawnbyahn koot uhn trahjheh jhewskah...?*
How far is it to...?	**C'est combien de kilomètres jusqu'à...?** *seh kawnbyahn duh keeloamehtr jhewskah...?*
Could you turn on the meter, please?	**Voulez-vous mettre le compteur en marche s'il vous plaît?** *voolay voo mehtr luh kawntuhr ohn mahrsh seel voo pleh?*
I'm in a hurry	**Je suis pressé.** *jhuh swee prehssay*
Could you speed up/slow down a little?	**Vous pouvez rouler plus vite/plus lentement?** *voo poovay roolay plew veet/plew lohntmohn?*
Could you take a different route?	**Vous pouvez prendre une autre route?** *voo poovay prohndr ewn oatr root?*

I'd like to get out here, please	**Je voudrais descendre ici** *jhuh voodreh duhsohndr eesee*
You have to go...here	**Là vous allez...** *lah voo zahlay...*
You have to go straight on here	**Là vous allez tout droit** *lah voo zahlay too drwah*
You have to turn left here	**Là vous allez à gauche** *lah voo zahlay zah goash*
You have to turn right here	**Là vous allez à droite** *lah voo zahlay zah drwaht*
This is it _____	**C'est ici** *seht eesee*
Could you wait a _____ minute for me, please?	**Vous pouvez m'attendre un instant?** *voo poovay mahtohndr uhn nahnstohn?*

7

Overnight accommodation

7.1 General

● **There is great variety** of overnight accommodation in France.
Hôtels: stars indicate the degree of comfort; from five stars, the most
luxurious, to one star, very simple. Beside the star one often finds the
letters NN-Nouvelles Normes (new classifications). This means that
the star-classification is up-to-date. Most hotels offer *pension
complète* (full board) or *demi-pension* (half board).
Auberges et Relais de campagne: luxurious; splendid view and lots
of rest are guaranteed.
Châteaux, Hôtels de France and Vieilles Demeures: a very expensive
tourist residence, always within a castle, country manor or an historic
building.
Logis de France: an organisation with many hotels with one or two
stars, mostly outside the town centre. The hotel can be recognised
by the yellow signboards with a green fireplace and the words: logis
de France.
Motels: especially along the motorway, comparable to UK motels.
Auberges de jeunesse (youth hostel): the number of nights is
restricted to between three and seven.
Camping: free camping is allowed, except for forest areas with the
sign *attention au feu* (fire hazard). Not all camping sites are guarded.
Refuges et gîtes d'étape (mountain huts): in the Alps and Pyrenees.
These huts are owned by the *Club Alpin Français* and are
inexpensive.

Combien de temps voulez-vous rester?	How long do you want to stay?
Voulez-vous remplir ce questionnaire s'il vous plaît?	Fill out this form, please
Puis-je avoir votre passeport?	Could I see your passport?
Vous devez payer un acompte	I'll need a deposit
Vous devez payer à l'avance	You'll have to pay in advance

My name's...I've made a reservation over the phone/by mail	Mon nom est...J'ai réservé une place par téléphone/par lettre
	mawn nawn eh...jhay rayzehrvay ewn plahs pahr taylayfon/pahr lehtr
How much is it per night/week/ month?	Quel est le prix pour une nuit/une semaine/un mois?
	kehl eh luh pree poor ewn nwee/ewn suhmehn/uhn mwah?
We'll be staying at least...nights/weeks	Nous restons au moins...nuits/semaines.
	noo rehstawn zoa mwhan...nwee/suhmehn
We don't know yet	Nous ne le savons pas encore exactement.
	noo nuh luh sahvawn pah zohnkor ehgzahktmohn
Do you allow pets (cats/dogs)?	Est-ce que les animaux domestiques(chiens/chats) sont admis?
	ehs kuh lay zahneemoa domehsteek(shyahn/shah) sawn tahdmee?
What time does the gate/door open/close?	A quelle heure on ouvre/ferme le portail/la porte?
	ah keh uhr awn noovr/fehrm luh portahy/lah port?
Could you get me a taxi, please?	Vous voulez m'appeler un taxi?
	voo voolay mahplay uhn tahksee?
Is there any mail for me?	Y a-t-il du courrier pour moi?
	ee yah teel dew kooryay poor mwah?

7.2 Camping

Where's the manager?	Où est le gardien?
	oo eh luh gahrdyahn?
Are we allowed to camp here?	Pouvons-nous camper ici?
	poovawn noo kohnpay eesee?

Vous pouvez vous-même choisir votre emplacement.	You can pick your own site
Votre emplacement vous sera attribué.	You'll be allocated a site
Voici votre numéro d'emplacement.	This is your site number
Vous devez coller ceci sur votre voiture.	Stick this on your car, please
Ne perdez surtout pas cette carte.	Please don't lose this card

There are...of us and ___ ...tents
Nous sommes...personnes et nous avons...tentes.
noo som...pehrson ay nooz ahvawn...tohnt

Can we pick our_____ own place?
Pouvons-nous choisir nous-mêmes un emplacement?
poovawn noo shwahzeer noo mehm uhn nohnplahsmohn?

Do you have a quiet ___ spot for us?
Avez-vous un endroit calme pour nous?
ahvay voo zuhn nohndrwah kahlm poor noo?

Do you have any other _ pitches available?
Vous n'avez pas d'autre emplacement libre?
voo nahvay pah doatr ohnplahsmohn leebr?

It's too windy/sunny/ ___ shady here.
Ici il y a trop de vent/soleil/ombre.
eesee eel ee yah troa duh vohn/sohlehy/awnbr

It's too crowded here ___
Il y a trop de monde ici.
eel ee yah troa duh mawnd eesee

The ground's too _____ hard/uneven
Le sol est trop dur/irrégulier.
luh sohl eh troa dewr/eeraygewlyay

Do you have a level ____ spot for the camper/caravan/folding caravan?	Avez-vous un endroit plat pour le camping-car/la caravane/la caravane pliante?
	ahvay voo zuhn nohndrwah plah poor luh kohnpeeng kahr/lah kahrahvahnn/lah kahrahvahnn plyohnt?
Could we have ____ adjoining pitches?	Pouvons-nous être l'un à côté de l'autre?
	poovawn noo zehtr luhn nah koatay duh loatr?
Can we park the car ____ next to the tent?	La voiture, peut-elle être garée à côté de la tente?
	lah vwahtewr, puh tehl ehtr gahray ah koatay duh lah tohnt?
How much is it per ____ person/tent/caravan/car?	Quel est le prix par personne/tente/caravane/voiture?
	kehl eh luh pree pahr pehrson/tohnt/kahrahvahnn/vwahtewr?
Are there any...? ____	Y a-t-il...?
	ee yah teel...?
– any hot showers? ____	Y a-t-il des douches avec eau chaude?
	ee yah teel day doosh ahvehk oa shoad?
– washing machines? __	Y a-t-il des machines à laver?
	ee yah teel day mahsheen ah lahvay?
Is there a...on the site? _	Y a-t-il un...sur le terrain?
	ee ayh teel uhn...sewr luh tehrahn?
Is there a children's ____ play area on the site?	Y a-t-il un terrain de jeux pour les enfants?
	ee yah teel uhn tehrahn duh jhuh poor lay zohnfohn?
Are there covered ____ cooking facilities on the site?	Y a-t-il un endroit couvert pour cuisiner?
	ee yah teel uhn nohndrwa koovehr poor kweezeenay?
Can I rent a safe here? _	Puis-je louer un coffre-fort ici?
	pwee jhuh looay uhn kofr for eesee?
Are we allowed to ____ barbecue here?	Pouvons-nous faire un barbecue?
	poovawn noo fehr uhn bahrbuhkew?

Are there any power points?	Y a-t-il des prises électriques?
	ee yah teel day preez aylehktreek?
Is there drinking water?	Y a-t-il de l'eau potable?
	ee yah teel duh loa potabl?
When's the rubbish collected?	Quand vide-t-on les poubelles?
	kohn veed-uh-tawn lay poobehl?
Do you sell gas bottles (butane gas/propane gas)?	Vendez-vous des bouteilles de gaz (butane/propane)?
	vohnday voo day bootehuhy duh gahz (bewtahnn/propahnn)?

7.3 Hotel/B&B/apartment/holiday house

Do you have a single/double room available?	Avez-vous une chambre libre pour une personne/deux personnes?
	ahvay voo zewn shohnbr leebr poor ewn pehrson/duh pehrson?
per person/per room	par personne/par chambre
	pahr pehrson/pahr shohnbr
Does that include breakfast/lunch/ dinner?	Est-ce que le petit déjeuner/le déjeuner/le dîner est compris?
	ehs kuh luh puhtee dayjhuhnay/luh dayjhuhnay/luh deenay eh kawnpree?
Could we have two adjoining rooms?	Pouvons-nous avoir deux chambres contiguës?
	poovawn noo zahvwahr duh shohnbr kawnteegew?
with/without toilet/bath/shower	avec/sans toilettes/salle de bains/douche
	ahvehk/sohn twahleht/sahl duh bahn/doosh
(not) facing the street	(pas) du côté rue
	(pah) dew koatay rew
with/without a view of the sea	avec/sans vue sur la mer
	ahvehk/sohn vew sewr lah mehr

Camping equipment

luggage space	l'espace (f.) bagages	*lehspahs bahgajh*
can opener	l'ouvre-boîte (m.)	*loovr bwaht*
butane gas bottle	la bouteille de butane	*lah bootehy duh bewtahnn*
pannier	la sacoche de vélo	*lah sahkosh duh vayloa*
gas cooker	le réchaud à gaz	*luh rayshoa ah gahz*
groundsheet	le tapis de sol	*luh tahpee duh sol*
mallet	le marteau	*luh mahrtoa*
hammock	le hamac	*luh ahmahk*
jerry can	le bidon d'essence	*luh beedawn dehssohns*
campfire	le feu de camp	*luh fuh duh kohn*
folding chair	la chaise pliante	*lah shehz plyohnt*
insulated picnic box	la glacière	*lah glahsyehr*
ice pack	le bac à glaçons	*luh bah kah glasawn*
compass	la boussole	*lah boosol*
wick	la mèche	*lah mehsh*
corkscrew	le tire-bouchon	*luh teer booshawn*
airbed	le matelas pneumatique	*luh mahtuhlah pnuhmahteek*
airbed plug	le bouchon du matelas pneumatique	*luh booshawn dew mahtuhlah pnemahteek*
pump	la pompe à air	*lah pawnp ah ehr*

| Is there...in the hotel? __ | Y a-t-il...dans l'hôtel? *ee yah teel...dohn loatehl?* |
| Is there a lift in the _____ hotel? | Y a-t-il un ascenseur dans l'hôtel? *ee yah teel uhn nahsohnsuhr dohn loatehl?* |

awning	l'auvent (m.)	loavohn
karimat	la natte	lah naht
pan	la casserole	lah kahsrol
pan handle	la poignée de casserole	lah pwahnnyay duh kahsrol
primus stove	le réchaud à pétrole	luh rayshoa ah paytrol
zip	la fermeture éclair	lah fehrmuhtewr ayklehr
backpack	le sac à dos	luh sahk ah doa
guy rope	la corde	lah kord
sleeping bag	le sac de couchage	luh sahk duh kooshajh
storm lantern	a lanterne-tempête	lah lohntehrn-tohnpeht
camp bed	e lit de camp	luh lee duh kohn
table	la table	lah tahbl
tent	la tente	lah tohnt
tent peg	le piquet	luh peekeh
tent pole	le mât	luh mah
vacuum flask	la bouteille thermos	lah bootehy tehrmos
water bottle	la gourde	lah goord
clothes peg	la pince à linge	lah pahns ah lahnjh
windbreak	le pare-vent	luh pahrvohn
torch	la torche électrique	lah torsh aylehktreek
pocket knife	le canif	luh kahneef

Do you have room _____ service?	Y a-t-il un service de chambre dans l'hôtel?
	ee yah teel uhn sehrvees duh shohnbr dohn loatehl?

Les toilettes et la douche sont au même étage/dans votre chambre	You can find the toilet and shower on the same floor/en suite
De ce côté, s'il vous plaît	This way, please
Votre chambre est au...étage, c'est le numéro...	Your room is on the...floor, number...

Could I see the room? — Puis-je voir la chambre?
pwee jhuh vwhar lah shohnbr?

I'll take this room ____ Je prends cette chambre.
jhuh prohn seht shohnbr

We don't like this one ___ Celle-ci ne nous plaît pas.
sehl see nuh noo pleh pah

Do you have a larger/ ___ Avez-vous une chambre plus
less expensive room? grande/moins chère?
avay voo zewn shohnbr plew grohnd/mwahn shehr?

Could you put in a ____ Pouvez-vous y ajouter un lit d'enfant?
cot? *poovay voo zee ahjhootay uhn lee dohnfohn?*

What time's _____ A quelle heure est le petit déjeuner?
breakfast? *ah kehl uhr eh luh puhtee dayjhuhnay?*

Where's the dining _____ Où est la salle à manger?
room? *oo eh lah sahl ah mohnjhay?*

Can I have breakfast ___ Puis-je prendre le petit déjeuner dans la
in my room? chambre?
pwee jhuh prohndr luh puhtee dayjhuhnay dohn lah shohnbr?

Where's the _____ Où est la sortie de secours/l'escalier de
emergency exit/fire secours?
escape? *oo eh lah sortee duh suhkoor/lehskahlyay duh suhkoor?*

Where can I park my ___ car (safely)?	Où puis-je garer ma voiture (en sécurité)?
	oo pwee jhuh gahray mah vwahtewr (ohn saykewreetay)?
The key to room...,____ please	La clef de la chambre..., s'il vous plaît.
	lah klay duh lah shohnbr...,seel voo pleh
Could you put this in ___ the safe, please?	Puis-je mettre ceci dans votre coffre-fort?
	pwee jhuh mehtr suhsee dohn votr kofr for?
Could you wake me____ at...tomorrow?	Demain voulez-vous me réveiller à...heures?
	duhmahn voolay voo muh rayvehyay ah...uhr?
Could you find a_____ babysitter for me?	Pouvez-vous m'aider à trouver une baby-sitter?
	poovay voo mayday ah troovay ewn behbee seetehr?
Could I have an extra __ blanket?	Puis-je avoir une couverture supplémentaire?
	pwee jhahvwahr ewn koovehrtewr sewplaymohntehr?
What days do the_____ cleaners come in?	Quels jours fait-on le ménage?
	kehl jhoor feh tawn luh maynahjh?
When are the sheets/ __ towels/tea towels changed?	Quand change-t-on les draps/les serviettes-éponge/les torchons?
	kohn shohnjh tawn lay drah/lay sehrvyeht aypawnjh/lay tohrshawn?

7.4 Complaints

| We can't sleep for _____ the noise | Nous ne pouvons pas dormir à cause du bruit |
| | *noo nuh poovawn pah dormeer ah koaz dew brwee* |

Could you turn the _____ radio down, please?	Est-ce que vous pouvez baisser un peu la radio?
	ehs kuh voo poovay behssay uhn puh lah rahdyoa?
We're out of toilet _____ paper	Il n'y a plus de papier hygiénique
	eel nee yah plew duh pahpyay eejhyayneek
There aren't _____ any.../there's not enough...	Il n'y a pas de/pas assez de...
	eel nee yah pah duh/pah zahsay duh...
The bed linen's dirty _____	La literie est sale
	lah leetree eh sahl
The room hasn't been _____ cleaned	La chambre n'a pas été nettoyée
	lah shohnbr nah pah zayatay nehtwahyay
The kitchen is not _____ clean	La cuisine n'est pas propre
	lah kweezeen neh pah propr
The kitchen utensils _____ are dirty	Les ustensiles de cuisine sont sales
	lay zewstohnseel duh kweezeen sawn sahl
The heater's not _____ working	Le chauffage ne marche pas
	luh shoafajh nuh marsh pah
There's no (hot) _____ water/electricity	Il n'y a pas d'eau(chaude)/d'électricité
	eel nee yah pah doa(shoad)/daylehktreeseetay
...is broken _____	...est cassé
	...eh kahssay
Could you have that _____ seen to?	Vous pouvez le faire réparer?
	voo poovay luh fehr raypahray?
Could I have another _____ room/site?	Puis-je avoir une autre chambre/un autre emplacement pour la tente?
	pwee jhuh ahvwahr ewn oatr shohnbr/uhn noatr ohnplasmohn poor lah tohnt?
The bed creaks terribly _____	Le lit grince énormément
	luh lee grahns aynormaymohn
The bed sags _____	Le lit s'affaisse
	luh lee sahfehs

There are bugs/insects in our room	Nous sommes incommodés par des bestioles/insectes *noo som zahnkomoday pahr day behstyol/day zahnsehkt*
This place is full of mosquitos	C'est plein de moustiques ici *seh plahn duh moosteek eesee*
– cockroaches	C'est plein de cafards *seh plahn duh kahfahr*

7.5 Departure

See also 8.2 Settling the bill

I'm leaving tomorrow. Could I settle my bill, please?	Je pars demain. Puis-je payer maintenant? *jhuh pahr duhmahn. pwee jhuh payay mahntuhnohn?*
What time should we vacate?	A quelle heure devons-nous quitter la chambre? *ah kehl uhr duhvawn noo keetay lah shohnbr?*
Could I have my passport back, please?	Pouvez-vous me rendre mon passeport? *poovay voo muh rohndr mawn pahspor?*
We're in a terrible hurry	Nous sommes très pressés *noo som treh prehssay*
Could you forward my mail to this address?	Pouvez-vous faire suivre mon courrier à cette adresse? *poovay voo fehr sweevr mawn kooryay ah seht ahdrehs?*
Could we leave our luggage here until we leave?	Nos valises peuvent rester ici jusqu'à notre départ? *noa vahleez puhv rehstay eesee jhewskah notr daypahr?*
Thanks for your hospitality	Merci pour votre hospitalité *mehrsee poor votr ospeetahleetay*

8

Money matters

● **In general**, banks are open 9–12 and 2–4pm; they are closed on Saturdays. In city centres they are often open at lunchtime. In tourist areas, the bank can be closed on Monday morning and open on Saturday morning. To exchange currency a proof of identity is usually required. The sign *Change* indicates that money can be exchanged.

8.1 Banks

Where can I find a ____ bank/an exchange office around here?	Où puis-je trouver une banque/un bureau de change par ici? *oo pwee jhuh troovay ewn bohnk/uhn bewroa duh shohnjh pahr eesee?*
Where can I cash this ___ traveller's cheque/giro cheque?	Où puis-je encaisser ce chèque de voyage/chèque postal? *oo pwee jhuh ohnkehssay suh shehk duh vwahyajh/shehk postahl?*
Can I cash this...here? _	Puis-je encaisser ce...ici? *pweejh ohnkehssay suh...eesee?*
Can I withdraw money _ on my credit card here?	Puis-je retirer de l'argent avec une carte de crédit? *pwee jhuh ruhteeray duh lahrjhohn ahvehk ewn kahrt duh kraydee?*
What's the minimum/ __ maximum amount?	Quel est le montant minimum/maximum? *kehl eh luh mohntohn meeneemuhm/mahxseemuhm?*
Can I take out less____ than that?	Puis-je retirer moins? *pwee jhuh ruhteeray mwahn?*
I've had some money __ transferred here. Has it arrived yet?	J'ai fait virer de l'argent par mandat télégraphique. Est-ce déjà arrivé? *jhay feh veeray duh lahrjhohn pahr mohndah taylaygrahfeek. ehs dayjhah ahreevay?*
These are the details___ of my bank in the UK	Voici les coordonnées de ma banque au Royaume-Uni *vwahsee lay koa-ordonay duh mah bohnk oa rwahyoam ewnee*

Vous devez signer ici	You have to sign here
Vous devez remplir ceci	You have to fill this out
Puis-je voir votre passeport?	Could I see your passport?
Puis-je voir une pièce d'identité?	Could I see some identification?
Puis-je voir votre carte de chèque postal?	Could I see your girobank card?
Puis-je voir votre carte bancaire?	Could I see your bank card?

This is my bank/giro account number	Voici mon numéro de compte bancaire/numéro de chèque postal
	vwahsee mawn newmayroa duh kawnt bohnkehr/newmayroa duh shehk postahl
I'd like to change some money	J'aimerais changer de l'argent *jhehmuhreh shohnjhay duh lahrjhohn*
– pounds into...	des livres sterling contre... *day leevr stehrleeng kawntr...*
– dollars into...	des dollars contre... *day dolahr kawntr...*
What's the exchange rate?	Le change est à combien? *luh shohnjh eh tah kawnbyahn?*
Could you give me some small change with it?	Pouvez-vous me donner de la monnaie? *poovay voo muh donay duh lah moneh?*
This is not right	Ce n'est pas exact *suh neh pah zehgzah.*

8.2 Settling the bill

Could you put it on my bill?	Pouvez-vous le mettre sur mon compte? *poovay voo luh mehtr sewr mawn kawnt?*
Does this amount include service?	Est-ce que le service est compris(dans la somme)? *ehs kuh luh sehrvees eh kawnpree(dohn lah som)?*

Can I pay by...?	Puis-je payer avec…?
	pwee jhuh payay ahvehk...?
Can I pay by credit card?	Puis-je payer avec une carte de crédit?
	pwee jhuh payay ahvehk ewn kahrt duh kraydee?
Can I pay by traveller's cheque?	Puis-je payer avec un chèque de voyage?
	pwee jhuh payay ahvehk uhn shehk duh vwahyajh?
Can I pay with foreign currency?	Puis-je vous payer en devises étrangères?
	pwee jhuh voo payay ohn duhveez aytrohnjhehr?
You've given me too much/you haven't given me enough change	Vous m'avez trop/pas assez rendu
	voo mahvay troa/pah zahsay rohndew
Could you check this again, please?	Voulez-vous refaire le calcul?
	voolay voo ruhfehr luh kahlkewl?
Could I have a receipt, please?	Pouvez-vous me donner un reçu/le ticket de caisse?
	poovay voo muh donay uhn ruhsew/luh teekeh duh kehs?
I don't have enough money on me	Je n'ai pas assez d'argent sur moi
	jhuh nay pah zahsay dahrjhohn sewr mwah
This is for you	Voilà, c'est pour vous
	vwahlah seh poor voo
Keep the change	Gardez la monnaie
	gahrday lah moneh

Nous n'acceptons pas les cartes de crédit/les chèques de voyage/les devises étrangères	Credit cards/traveller's cheques/foreign currency are not accepted

9.1 Post

For giros, see 8 Money matters

● **Post offices** are open from Monday to Friday between 8am and 7pm. In smaller towns the post office closes at lunch. On Saturday they are open between 8am and 12 noon.
Stamps *(timbres)* are also available in a *tabac* (café that sells cigarettes and matches).
The yellow letter box *(boîte aux lettres)* in the street and in the post office has two rates: *tarif normal* (normal rate) and *tarif réduit* (reduced rate).
It is advisable to opt for the *tarif normal.*

colis	télégrammes	timbres
parcels	telegrams	stamps
mandats		
money orders		

Where's...?	Où est...?
	oo eh...?
Where's the post office?	Où est la poste?
	oo eh lah post?
Where's the main post office?	Où est la poste centrale?
	oo eh lah post sohntrahl?
Where's the postbox?	Où est la boîte aux lettres?
	oo eh lah bwaht oa lehtr?
Which counter should I go to...?	Quel est le guichet pour...?
	kehl eh luh gueesheh poor...?
– to send a fax	Quel est le guichet pour les fax?
	kehl eh luh gueesheh poor lay fahx?

– to change money _____	Quel est le guichet pour changer de l'argent?
	kehl eh luh gueesheh poor shohnjhay duh lahrjhohn?
-to change giro _____ cheques	Quel est le guichet pour les chèques postaux?
	kehl eh luh gueesheh poor lay shehk postoa?
-for a telegraph money _ order?	Quel est le guichet pour faire un virement postal télégraphique?
	kehl eh luh gueesheh poor fehr uhn veermohn postahl taylaygrahfeek?
Poste restante _____	Poste restante
	post rehstohnt
Is there any mail for_____ me? My name's...	Y a-t-il du courrier pour moi? Mon nom est...
	ee yah teel dew kooryay poor mwah? mawn nawn eh...

Stamps

What's the postage _____ for a...to...?	Combien faut-il sur une...pour...?
	kawnbyahn foa teel sewr ewn...poor...?
Are there enough _____ stamps on it?	Y a-t-il suffisamment de timbres dessus?
	ee yah teel sewfeezahmohn duh tahnbr duhsew?
I'd like... ...euro_____ stamps	Je voudrais...timbres à...
	jhuh voodreh...tahnbr ah...
I'd like to send this... ___	Je veux envoyer ce/cette...
	jhuh vuh zohnvwahyay suh/seht...
– express _____	Je veux envoyer ce/cette...en express.
	jhuh vuh zohnvwahyay suh/seht...ohn nehxprehs
– by air mail_____	Je veux envoyer ce/cette...par avion.
	jhuh vuh zohnvwahyay suh/seht...pahr ahvyawn

| – by registered mail ____ | Je veux envoyer ce/cette...en recommandé. |
| | *jhuh vuh zohnvwahyay suh/seht...ohn ruhkomohnday* |

Telegram / fax

I'd like to send a_____ telegram to...	J'aimerais envoyer un télégramme à...
	jhehmuhreh zohnvwahyay uhn taylaygrahm ah...
How much is that_____ per word?	C'est combien par mot?
	seh kawnbyahn pahr moa?
This is the text I want __ to send	Voici le texte que je veux envoyer.
	vwahsee luh tehxt kuh jhuh vuh zohnvwahyay
Shall I fill out the form __ myself?	Puis-je remplir le questionnaire moi-même?
	pwee jhuh rohnpleer luh kehstyonehr mwah mehm?
Can I make _____ photocopies/ send a fax here?	Puis-je faire des photocopies/envoyer un fax ici?
	pwee jhuh fehr day foatoakopee/ ohnvwahyay uhn fahx eesee?

9.2 Telephone

See also 1.8 Telephone alphabet

● All phone booths offer a direct international service to the UK or the US (00 + country code 44[UK] or 1[US]+ trunk code minus zero + number). Most phone booths will only accept phone cards *(télécartes)*, which can be bought at the post office or in a *tabac*. Phone booths do not take incoming calls. Charges can no longer be reversed in France. A *carte globéo* (special card) can be obtained from any office of the telephone company, on presentation of a credit card and identification. Charges are then deducted from the bank account. When phoning someone in France, you will not be greeted with the subscriber's name, but with *allô* or *allô oui?*

Is there a phone box ___ around here?	Y a-t-il une cabine téléphonique dans le coin? *ee ah teel ewn kahbeen taylayfoneek dohn luh kwahn?*
Could I use your_____ phone, please?	Puis-je utiliser votre téléphone? *pwee jhuh ewteeleezay votr taylayfon?*
Do you have a _____ (city/region)...phone directory?	Avez-vous un annuaire de la ville de.../de la région de...? *ahvay voo zuhn ahnnewehr duh lah veel duh.../duh lah rayjhyawn duh...?*
Where can I get a_____ phone card?	Où puis-je acheter une télécarte? *oo pwee jhahshtay ewn taylaykahrt?*
Could you give me...? __	Pouvez-vous me donner...? *poovay voo muh donay...?*
– the number for_____ international directory enquiries	Pouvez-vous me donner le numéro des renseignements pour l'étranger? *poovay voo muh donay luh newmayroa day rohnsehnyuhmohn poor laytrohnjhay?*
– the number of _____ room...	Pouvez-vous me donner le numéro de la chambre...? *poovay voo muh donay luh newmayroa duh lah shohnbr...?*
– the international _____ access code	Pouvez-vous me donner le numéro international? *poovay voo muh donay luh newmayroa ahntehrnahsyonahl?*
– the country code_____ for...	Pouvez-vous me donner l'indicatif du pays pour...? *poovay voo muh donay lahndeekahteef dew payee poor...?*
– the trunk code for... __	Pouvez-vous me donner l'indicatif de...? *poovay voo muh donay lahndeekahteef duh...?*
– the number of..._____	Pouvez-vous me donner le numéro d'abonné de...? *poovay voo muh donay luh newmayroa dahbonay duh...?*

Could you check if this this number's correct?	Pouvez-vous vérifier si ce numéro est correct? *poovay voo vayreefyay see suh newmayroa eh korehkt?*
Can I dial international direct?	Puis-je téléphoner en automatique à l'étranger? *pwee jhuh taylayfonay ohn noatoamahteek ah laytrohnjhay?*
Do I have to go through the switchboard?	Dois-je appeler en passant par le standard? *dwah jhahpuhlay ohn pahsohn pahr luh stohndahr?*
Do I have to dial '0' first?	Dois-je d'abord faire le zéro? *dwah jhuh dahbor fehr luh zayroa?*
Do I have to book my calls?	Dois-je demander ma communication? *dwah jhuh duhmohnday mah komewneekahsyawn?*
Could you dial this number for me, please?	Voulez-vous m'appeler ce numéro? *voolay voo mahpuhlay suh newmayroa?*
Could you put me through to.../ extension..., please?	Voulez-vous me passer.../le poste...? *voolay voo muh pahsay.../luh post...?*
What's the charge per minute?	Quel est le prix à la minute? *kehl eh luh pree ah lah meenewt?*
Have there been any calls for me?	Quelqu'un m'a-t-il appelé? *kehlkuhn mah teel ahpuhlay?*

The conversation

Hello, this is...	Allô, ici... *ahloa, eesee...*
Who is this, please?	Qui est à l'appareil? *kee eh tah lahpahrehy?*
Is this...?	Je parle à...? *jhuh pahrl ah...?*
I'm sorry, I've dialled the wrong number	Pardon, je me suis trompé(e) de numéro *pahrdawn, jhuh muh swee trawnpay duh newmayroa.*

I can't hear you_____	Je ne vous entends pas
	jhuh nuh voo zohntohn pah
I'd like to speak to... ___	Je voudrais parler à...
	jhuh voodreh pahrlay ah...
Is there anybody_____ who speaks English?	Y a-t-il quelqu'un qui parle l'anglais?
	ee yah teel kehlkuhn kee pahrl lohngleh?
Extension... please_____	Pouvez-vous me passer le poste...?
	poovay voo muh pahsay luh post...?
Could you ask_____ him/her to call me back?	Voulez-vous demander qu'il/qu'elle me rappelle?
	voolay voo duhmohnday keel/kehl muh rahpehl?
My name's... _____ My number's...	Mon nom est...Mon numéro est...
	mawn nawn eh...mawn newmayroa eh...
Could you tell him/her __ I called?	Voulez-vous dire que j'ai appelé?
	voolay voo deer kuh jhay ahpuhlay?
I'll call back tomorrow	Je rappellerai demain
	jhuh rahpehluhray duhmah

On vous demande au téléphone	There's a phone call for you
Vous devez d'abord faire le zéro	You have to dial '0' first
Vous avez un instant?	One moment, please
Je n'obtiens pas de réponse	There's no answer
La ligne est occupée	The line's engaged
Vous voulez attendre?	Could you hold?
Je vous passe la communication	Putting you through
Vous vous êtes trompé de numéro	You've got the wrong number
Il/elle n'est pas ici en ce moment	He's/she's not here right now
Vous pouvez le/la rappeler à...	He'll/she'll be back...
C'est le répondeur automatique de...	This is the answering machine of...

10 Shopping

● **Opening times:** Tuesday to Saturday 8/9am–1pm and 2.30–7pm. On Mondays shops are closed in the morning or for the entire day. On Sunday mornings grocers and bakers are usually open, and markets are open until 1pm. Supermarkets and department stores in nearly all cities are open until 8pm once a week. Chemists display the list of *pharmacies de garde* (those open on Sundays and after hours), but you may be charged double in some cities. You may be asked to pay in advance for shoe repairs and dry cleaning.

10.1 Shopping conversations

Where can I get...?	Dans quel magasin puis-je acheter...?
	dohn kehl mahgahzahn pwee jhahshtay...?
When does this shop open?	A quelle heure ouvre ce magasin?
	ah kehl uhr oovr suh mahgahzahn?
Could you tell me where the...department is?	Pouvez-vous m'indiquer le rayon de...?
	poovay voo mahndeekay luh rayawn duh...?
Could you help me, please? I'm looking for...	Pouvez-vous m'aider? Je cherche...
	poovay voo mayday? jhuh shehrsh...
Do you sell English/ American newspapers?	Vendez-vous des journaux anglais/américains?
	vohnday voo day jhoornoa ohngleh/ahmayreekahn?

On s'occupe de vous?	Are you being served?

No, I'd like...	Non. J'aimerais...
	nawn. jhehmuhreh...
I'm just looking, if that's all right	Je jette un coup d'oeil, si c'est permis
	jhuh jheht uhn koo duhy, see seh pehrmee

antiquités antiques
appareils électriques electrical appliances
bijoutier jeweller
blanchisserie laundry
boucherie butcher
boulangerie bakery
centre commercial shopping centre
charcuterie delicatessen
coiffeur (femmes/hommes) hairdresser (women/men)
cordonnier cobbler
crémerie dairy
épicerie grocery store
fleuriste florist
fruits et légumes greengrocer
galerie marchande shopping arcade
grand magasin department store

laverie automatique launderette
librairie bookshop
magasin shop
magasin d'ameublement furniture shop
magasin d'appareils photographiques camera shop
magasin de bicyclettes bicycle shop
magasin de bricolage DIY-store
magasin de jouets toy shop
magasin de disques record shop
magasin de souvenirs souvenir shop
magasin de sport sports shop
magasin de vins et spiritueux off-licence

magasin diététique health food shop
marché market
marché aux puces fleamarket
mercerie draper
pâtisserie cake shop
pharmacie chemist
poissonnerie fishmonger
produits ménagers/ droguerie household goods
quincaillerie hardware shop
réparateur de bicyclettes bicycle repairs
salon de beauté beauty parlour
salon de dégustation de glaces ice-cream parlour
supermarché supermarket
tabac tobacconist
teinturerie dry-cleaner

Vous désirez autre chose?   Anything else?

Yes, I'd also like... _____   Oui, donnez-moi aussi...
                                wee, donay mwah oasee...

No, thank you _____ That's all	Non, je vous remercie. Ce sera tout *nawn, jhuh voo ruhmehrsee. suh suhrah too*
Could you show me...?	Pouvez-vous me montrer...? *poovay voo muh mawntray…?*
I'd prefer... _____	Je préfère... *jhuh prayfehr…*
This is not what I'm ____ looking for	Ce n'est pas ce que je cherche *suh neh pah suh kuh jhuh shehrsh*
Thank you. I'll keep ____ looking	Merci. Je chercherai ailleurs *mehrsee. jhuh shehrshuhray ahyuhr*
Do you have _____ something...?	Vous n'avez pas quelque chose de...? *voo nahvay pah kehlkuh shoaz duh…?*
– less expensive? _____	Vous n'avez pas quelque chose de moins cher? *voo nahvay pah kehlkuh shoaz duh mwahn shehr?*
– something smaller? __	Vous n'avez pas quelque chose de plus petit? *voo nahvay pah kehlkuh shoaz duh plew puhtee?*
– something larger? ____	Vous n'avez pas quelque chose de plus grand? *voo nahvay pah kehlkuh shoaz duh plew grohn?*
I'll take this one _____	Je prends celui-ci *jhuh prohn suhlwee see*
Does it come with ____ instructions?	Y a-t-il un mode d'emploi avec? *ee yah teel uhn mod dohnplwah ahvehk?*
It's too expensive _____	Je le trouve trop cher *jhuh luh troov troa shehr*
I'll give you... _____	Je vous offre... *jhuh voo zofr…*
Could you keep this ___ for me? I'll come back for it later	Voulez-vous me le mettre de côté? Je reviendrai le chercher tout à l'heure *voolay voo muh luh mehtr duh koatay? jhuh ruhvyahndray luh shehrshay too tah luhr*

Je suis désolé, nous n'en avons pas	I'm sorry, we don't have that
Je suis désolé, le stock est épuisé	I'm sorry, we're sold out
Je suis désolé, ce ne sera pas livré avant...	I'm sorry, that won't be in until...
Vous pouvez payer à la caisse	You can pay at the cash desk
Nous n'acceptons pas les cartes de crédit	We don't accept credit cards
Nous n'acceptons pas les chèques de voyage	We don't accept traveller's cheques
Nous n'acceptons pas les devises étrangères	We don't accept foreign currency

Have you got a bag for me, please?	Vous avez un sac?
	voo zahvay uhn sahk?
Could you giftwrap it, please?	Vous pouvez l'emballer dans un papier cadeau?
	voo poovay lohnbahlay dohn zuhn pahpyay kahdoa?

10.2 Food

I'd like a hundred grams of..., please	Je voudrais cent grammes de...
	jhuh voodreh sohn grahm duh...
– five hundred grams/ half a kilo of...	Je voudrais une livre de...
	jhuh voodreh zewn leevr duh...
– a kilo of...	Je voudrais un kilo de...
	jhuh voodreh zuhn keeloa duh...
Could you...it for me, please?	Vous voulez me le...?
	voo voolay muh luh...?

Could you slice it/ dice it for me, please?	Vous voulez me le couper en tranches/morceaux?
	voo voolay muh luh koopay ohn trohnsh/mohrsoa?
Could you grate it for me, please?	Vous voulez me le râper?
	voo voolay muh luh rahpay?
Can I order it?	Puis-je le commander?
	pwee jhuh luh komohnday?
I'll pick it up tomorrow/ at...	Je viendrai le chercher demain/à...heures
	jhuh vyahndray luh shehrshay duhmahn/ah...uhr
Can you eat/drink this?	Est-ce mangeable/buvable?
	ehs mohnjhahbl/bewvahbl?
What's in it?	Qu'y a-t-il dedans?
	kee yah teel duhdohn?

10.3 Clothing and shoes

I saw something in the window. Shall I point it out?	J'ai vu quelque chose dans la vitrine. Je vous le montre?
	jhay vew kehlkuh shoaz dohn lah veetreen. jhuh voo lah mawntr?
I'd like something to go with this	J'aimerais quelque chose pour aller avec ceci
	jhehmuhreh kehlkuh shoaz poor ahlay ahvehk suhsee
Do you have shoes to match this?	Avez-vous des chaussures de la même couleur que ça?
	ahvay voo day shoasewr duh lah mehm kooluhr kuh sah?
I'm a size...in the UK	Je fais du...au Royaume-Uni
	jhuh feh dew...oa rwahyoam ewnee
Can I try this on?	Puis-je l'essayer?
	pwee jhuh lehsayay?
Where's the fitting room?	Où est la cabine d'essayage?
	oo eh lah kahbeen dehsayahjh?

Ne pas repasser Do not iron	Nettoyage à sec Dry clean	Étendre humide Drip dry
Laver à la main Hand wash	Ne pas essorer Do not spin dry	Laver à la machine Machine wash

It doesn't fit_____ Cela ne me va pas
suhlah nuh muh vah pah

This is the right size____ C'est la bonne taille
seh lah bon tahy

It doesn't suit me _____ Cela ne me convient pas
suhlah nuh muh kawnvyahn pah

Do you have this in...? _ L'avez-vous aussi en...?
lahvay voo zoasee ohn...?

The heel's too high/low_ Je trouve le talon trop haut/bas
jhuh troov luh tahlawn troa oa/bah

Is this/are these _____ Est-ce/sont-elles en cuir?
genuine leather? *eh suh/sawn tehl ohn kweer?*

I'm looking for a... _____ Je cherche un...pour un bébé/enfant
for a...-year-old   de...ans
baby/child *jhuh shehrsh uhn...poor uhn*
baybay/ohnhfohn duh...ohn

I'd like a... ... _____ J'aurais aimé un...de...
jhoareh zaymay uhn... duh...

– silk _____ J'aurais aimé un...de soie
jhoareh zaymay uhn...duh swah

– cotton _____ J'aurais aimé un...de coton
jhoareh zaymay uhn...duh koatawn

– woollen _____ J'aurais aimé un...de laine
jhoareh zaymay uhn...duh lehn

– linen_____ J'aurais aimé un...de lin
jhoareh zaymay uhn...duh lahn

What temperature _____ A quelle température puis-je le laver?
can I wash it at? *ah kehl tohnpayrahtewr pwee jhuh luh*
lahvay?

Will it shrink in the _____ Cela rétrécit au lavage?
wash? *suhlah raytraysee oa lahvahjh?*

123

At the cobbler

Could you mend_____ these shoes?	Pouvez-vous réparer ces chaussures?
	poovay voo raypahray say shoasewr?
Could you put new ____ soles/heels on these?	Pouvez-vous y mettre de nouvelles semelles/nouveaux talons?
	poovay voo zee mehtr duh noovehl suhmehl/noovoa tahlawn?
When will they be_____ ready?	Quand seront-elles prêtes?
	kohn suhrawn tehl preht?
I'd like..., please _____	Je voudrais...
	jhuh voodreh...
– a tin of shoe polish ___	Je voudrais une boîte de cirage
	jhuh voodreh zewn bwaht duh seerahjh
– a pair of shoelaces ___	Je voudrais une paire de lacets
	jhuh voodreh zewn pehr duh lahseh

10.4 Photographs and video

I'd like a film for this ___ camera, please	Je voudrais un rouleau de pellicules pour cet appareil
	jhuh voodreh zuhn rooloa duh payleekewl poor seht ahpahrehy
– a 126 _____ cartridge	Je voudrais une cartouche de cent vingt-six
	jhuh voodreh zewn kahrtoosh duh sohn vahn sees
– a slide film _____	Je voudrais un rouleau de pellicules pour diapositives
	jhuh voodreh zuhn rooloa duh payleekewl poor deeahpoaseeteev
– a film _____	Je voudrais un rouleau de pellicules
	jhuh voodreh zuhn rooloa duh payleekewl
– a videotape _____	Je voudrais une vidéocassette
	jhuh voodreh zewn veedayoakahseht

colour/black and white __	couleur/noir et blanc
	kooluhr/nwahr ay blohn
super eight _____	super huit mm
	sewpehr wee meeleemehtr
12/24/36 exposures____	douze/vingt-quatre/trente-six poses
	dooz/vahn kahtr/trohnt see poaz
ASA/DIN number _____	nombre d'ASA/DIN
	nohnbr dahzah/deen
daylight film_____	film pour la lumière du jour
	feelm poor lah lewmyehr dew joor
film for artificial light ___	film pour la lumière artificielle
	feelm poor lah lewmyehr ahrteefeesyehl

Problems

Could you load the _____ film for me, please?	Voulez-vous mettre le film dans l'appareil?
	voolay voo mehtr luh feelm dohn lahpahrehy?
Could you take the film_ out for me, please?	Voulez-vous enlever le film de l'appareil-photo?
	voolay voo zohnluhvay luh feelm duh lahpahrehy foatoa?
Should I replace _____ the batteries?	Dois-je changer les piles?
	dwah jhuh shohnjhay lay peel?
Could you have a look _ at my camera, please? It's not working	Voulez-vous jeter un coup d'oeil à mon appareil-photo? Il ne marche plus
	voolay voo jhuhtay uhn koo duhy ah mawn nahpahrehy foatoa? eel nuh mahrsh plew
The...is broken _____	Le...est cassé
	luh...eh kahssay
The film's jammed _____	La pellicule est bloquée
	lah payleekewl eh blokay
The film's broken _____	La pellicule est cassée
	lah payleekewl eh kahssay
The flash isn't working _	Le flash ne marche pas
	luh flahsh nuh mahrsh pah

Processing and prints

I'd like to have this film developed/printed, please	Je voudrais faire développer/tirer ce film *jhuh voodreh fehr dayvuhlopay/teeray suh feelm*
I'd like...prints from ____ each negative	Je voudrais...tirages de chaque négatif *jhuh voodreh...teerahjh duh shahk naygahteef*
glossy/mat_____	brillant/mat *breeyohn/maht*
6x9 _____	six sur neuf *sees sewr nuhf*
I'd like to re-order ____ these photos	Je veux faire refaire cette photo *jhuh vuh fehr ruhfehr seht foatoa*
I'd like to have this____ photo enlarged	Je veux faire agrandir cette photo *jhuh vuh fehr ahgrohndeer seht foatoa*
How much is_____ processing?	Combien coûte le développement? *kawnbyahn koot luh dayvuhlopmohn?*
– printing _____	Combien coûte le tirage? *kawnbyahn koot luh teerahjh?*
– to re-order _____	Combien coûte la commande supplémentaire? *kawnbyahn koot lah komohnd sewplaymohntehr?*
– the enlargement ____	Combien coûte l'agrandissement? *kawnbyahn koot lahgrohndeesmohn?*
When will they _____ be ready?	Quand seront-elles prêtes? *kohn suhrawn tehl preht?*

10.5 At the hairdresser's

| Do I have to make an appointment? | Dois-je prendre un rendez-vous?
dwah jhuh prohndr uhn rohnday voo? |
| Can I come in straight away? | Pouvez-vous vous occuper de moi immédiatement?
poovay voo voo zokewpay duh mwah eemaydyahtmohn? |

How long will I have to wait?	Combien de temps dois-je attendre?
	kawnbyahn duh tohn dwah jhahtohndr?
I'd like a shampoo/ haircut	Je veux me faire laver/couper les cheveux
	jhuh vuh muh fehr lahvay/koopay lay shuhvuh
I'd like a shampoo for oily/dry hair, please	Je voudrais un shampooing pour cheveux gras/secs
	jhuh voodreh zuhn shohnpwahn poor shuhvuh grah/sehk
an anti-dandruff shampoo	Je voudrais un shampooing anti-pelliculaire
	jhuh voodreh zuhn shohnpwahn ohnteepayleekewlehr
– a shampoo for permed/coloured hair	Je voudrais un shampooing pour cheveux permanentés/colorés
	jhuh voodreh zuhn shohnpwahn poor shuhvuh pehrmahnohntay/kohlohray
– a colour rinse shampoo	Je voudrais un shampooing colorant
	jhuh voodreh zuhn shohnpwahn kolorohn
– a shampoo with conditioner	Je voudrais un shampoing avec un soin traitant
	jhuh voodreh zuhn shohnpwahn ahvehk uhn swahn trehtohn
– highlights	Je voudrais me faire faire des mèches
	jhuh voodreh muh fehr fehr day mehsh
Do you have a colour chart, please?	Avez-vous une carte de coloration s'il vous plaît?
	ahvay voo zewn kahrt duh kolorahsyawn seel voo pleh?
I want to keep it the same colour	Je veux garder la même couleur
	jhuh vuh gahrday lah mehm kooluhr
I'd like it darker/lighter	Je les veux plus sombres/clairs
	jhuh lay vuh plew sawmbr/klehr

I'd like/I don't want ____ hairspray	Je veux de la/ne veux pas de laque
	jhuh vuh duh la/nuh vuh pah duh lahk
– gel _____	Je veux du/ne veux pas de gel
	jhuh vuh dew/ nuh vuh pah duh jhehl
– lotion _____	Je veux de la/ne veux pas de lotion
	jhuh vuh duh lah/nuh vuh pah duh loasyawn
I'd like a short fringe ___	Je veux ma frange courte
	jhuh vuh mah frohnjh koort
Not too short at the ____ back	Je ne veux pas la nuque trop courte
	jhuh nuh vuh pah lah newk troa koort
Not too long here_____	Ici je ne les veux pas trop longs
	eesee jhuh nuh lay vuh pah troa lawn
I'd like/I don't want ____ (many) curls	Je (ne) veux (pas) être (trop) frisée
	jhuh (nuh) vuh (pah) ehtr (troa) freezay
It needs a little/_____ a lot taken off	Il faut en enlever une petite/grande quantité
	eel foa ohn nohnluhvay ewn puhteet/grohnd kohnteetay
I want a completely ____ different style	Je veux une toute autre coupe
	jhuh vuh zewn toot oatr koop
I'd like it like..._____	Je veux mes cheveux comme...
	jhuh vuh may shuhvuh kom...
– the same as that lady's _____	Je veux la même coiffure que cette femme
	jhuh vuh lah mehm kwahfewr kuh seht fahm
– the same as in this ___ photo	Je veux la même coiffure que sur cette photo
	jhuh vuh lah mehm kwahfewr kuh sewr seht foatoa
Could you put the _____ drier up/down a bit?	Pouvez-vous mettre le casque plus haut/plus bas?
	poovay voo mehtr luh kahsk plew oa/plew bah?
I'd like a facial_____	J'aimerais un masque de beauté
	jhehmuhreh zuhn mahsk duh boatay

Quelle coupe de cheveux désirez-vous?	How do you want it cut?
Quelle coiffure désirez-vous?	What style did you have in mind?
Quelle couleur désirez-vous?	What colour do you want it?
Est-ce la bonne température?	Is the temperature all right for you?
Voulez-vous lire quelque chose?	Would you like something to read?
Voulez-vous boire quelque chose?	Would you like a drink?
C'est ce que vous vouliez?	Is this what you had in mind?

– a manicure _____	J'aimerais qu'on me fasse les ongles *jhehmuhreh kawn muh fahs lay zawngl*
– a massage _____	J'aimerais un massage *jhehmuhreh zuhn mahsahjh*
Could you trim _____ my fringe?	Pouvez-vous égaliser ma frange? *poovay voo zaygahleezay mah frohnjh?*
– my beard? _____	Pouvez-vous égaliser ma barbe? *poovay voo zaygahleezay mah bahrb?*
– my moustache? _____	Pouvez-vous égaliser ma moustache? *poovay voo zaygahleezay mah moostahsh?*
I'd like a shave, please _	Pouvez-vous me raser s'il vous plaît? *poovay voo muh rahzay seel voo pleh?*
I'd like a wet shave, _____ please	Je veux être rasé au rasoir à main *jhuh vuh zehtr rahzay oa rahzwahr ah mahn*

129

11 At the Tourist Information Centre

11.1 Places of interest

Where's the Tourist Information, please? — Où est l'office de tourisme?
oo eh lofees duh tooreesm?

Do you have a city map? — Avez-vous un plan de la ville?
ahvay voo zuhn plohn duh lah veel?

Where is the museum? — Où est le musée?
oo eh luh mewzay?

Where can I find a church? — Où puis-je trouver une église?
oo pwee jhuh troovay ewn aygleez?

Could you give me some information about...? — Pouvez-vous me renseigner sur...?
poovay voo muh rohnsehnyay sewr...?

How much is that? — Combien ça coûte?
kawnbyahn sah koot?

What are the main places of interest? — Quelles sont les curiosités les plus importantes?
kehl sawn lay kewryoseetay lay plewz ahnportohnt?

Could you point them out on the map? — Pouvez-vous les indiquer sur la carte?
poovay voo lay zahndeekay sewr lah kahrt?

What do you recommend? — Que nous conseillez-vous?
kuh noo kawnsehyay voo?

We'll be here for a few hours — Nous restons ici quelques heures.
noo rehstawn zeesee kehlkuh zuhr.

– a day — Nous restons ici une journée.
noo rehstawn zeesee ewn jhoornay.

– a week — Nous restons ici une semaine.
noo rehstawn zeesee ewn suhmehn.

We're interested in... — Nous sommes intéressés par...
noo som zahntayrehsay pahr...

Is there a scenic walk around the city? — Pouvons-nous faire une promenade en ville?
poovawn noo fehr ewn promuhnahd ohn veel?

How long does it take?	Combien de temps dure-t-elle?
	kawnbyahn duh tohn dewr tehl?
Where does it _____ start/end?	Où est le point de départ/d'arrivée?
	oo eh luh pwahn duh daypahr/dahreevay?
Are there any boat _____ cruises here?	Y a-t-il des bateaux-mouches?
	ee yah teel day bahtoa moosh?
Where can we board? __	Où pouvons-nous embarquer?
	oo poovawn noo zohnbahrkay?
Are there any bus_____ tours?	Y a-t-il des promenades en bus?
	ee yah teel day promuhnahd ohn bews?
Where do we get on? __	Où devons-nous monter?
	oo devawn noo mawntay?
Is there a guide who ___ speaks English?	Y a-t-il un guide qui parle l'anglais?
	ee yah teel uhn gueed kee pahrl lohngleh?
What trips can we take_ around the area?	Quelles promenades peut-on faire dans la région?
	kehl promuhnahd puh tawn fehr dohn lah rayjhyawn?
Are there any_____ excursions?	Y a-t-il des excursions?
	ee yah teel day zehxkewrsyawn?
Where do they go to? __	Où vont-elles?
	oo vawn tehl?
We'd like to go to... ____	Nous voulons aller à...
	noo voolawn zahlay ah...
How long is the trip?___	Combien de temps dure l'excursion?
	kawnbyahn duh tohn dewr lehxkewrsyawn?
How long do we_____ stay in...?	Combien de temps restons-nous à...?
	kawnbyahn duh tohn rehstawn noo zah...?
Are there any guided___ tours?	Y a-t-il des visites guidées?
	ee yah teel day veezeet gueeday?
How much free time ___ will we have there?	Combien de temps avons-nous de libre?
	kawnbyahn duh tohn ahvawn noo duh leebr?
We want to go hiking___	Nous voulons faire une randonnée
	noo voolawn fehr ewn rohndonay
Can we hire a guide? __	Pouvons-nous prendre un guide?
	poovawn noo prohndr uhn gueed?

Can I book mountain huts?	Puis-je réserver un refuge?
	pwee jhuh rayzehrvay uhn ruhfewjhuh?
What time does... open/close?	A quelle heure ouvre/ferme...?
	ah kehl uhr oovr/fehrm...?
What days is...open/ closed?	Quels sont les jours d'ouverture/de fermeture de...?
	kehl sawn lay jhoor doovehrtewr/duh fehrmuhtewr duh...?
What's the admission price?	Quel est le prix d'entrée?
	kehl eh luh pree dohntray?
Is there a group discount?	Y a-t-il une réduction pour les groupes?
	ee yah teel ewn raydewksyawn poor lay groop?
Is there a child discount?	Y a-t-il une réduction pour les enfants?
	ee yah teel ewn raydewksyawn poor lay zohnfohn?
Is there a discount for pensioners?	Y a-t-il une réduction pour les personnes de plus de soixante-cinq ans?
	ee yah teel ewn raydewksyawn poor lay pehrson duh plew duh swahssohnt sahnk ohn?
Can I take (flash) photos/can I film here?	M'est-il permis de prendre des photos(avec flash)/filmer ici?
	meh teel pehrmee duh prohndr day foatoa(ahvehk flahsh)/feelmay eesee?
Do you have any postcards of...?	Vendez-vous des cartes postales de...?
	vohnday voo day kahrt postahl duh...?
Do you have an English...?	Avez-vous un...en anglais?
	ahvay voo zuhn...ohn nohngleh?
– an English catalogue?	Avez-vous un catalogue en anglais?
	ahvay voo zuhn kahtahlog ohn nohngleh?
– an English programme?	Avez-vous un programme en anglais?
	ahvay voo zuhn prograhm ohn nohngleh?
– an English brochure?	Avez-vous une brochure en anglais?
	ahvay voo zewn broshewr ohn nohngleh?

11.2 Going out

● **In French theatres** you are usually shown to your seat by an usherette from whom you can buy a programme. It is customary to tip. At the cinema most films are dubbed *(version française)*. In large cities subtitled versions are often screened, advertised as *version originale* or *V.O.* If the publicity does not mention *V.O.*, the film will be dubbed. *L'Officiel des spectacles* (an entertainment guide) can be obtained from newspaper kiosks

Do you have this _____ week's/month's entertainment guide?	Avez-vous le journal des spectacles de cette semaine/de ce mois? *ahvay voo luh jhoornal day spehktahkl duh seht suhmehn/duh suh mwah?*
What's on tonight? _____	Que peut-on faire ce soir? *kuh puh tawn fehr suh swahr?*
We want to go to... _____	Nous voulons aller au... *noo voolawn zahlay oa...*
Which films are _____ showing?	Quels films passe-t-on? *kehl feelm pah stawn?*
What sort of film is _____ that?	Qu'est-ce que c'est comme film? *kehs kuh seh kom feelm?*
suitable for all ages _____	pour tous les âges *poor too lay zahjh*
not suitable for _____ children under 12/16 years	pour les plus de douze ans/seize ans *poor lay plew duh dooz ohn/sehz ohn*
original version _____	version originale *vehrsyawn oreejheenahl*
subtitled _____	sous-titré *soo teetray*
dubbed _____	doublé *dooblay*
Is it a continuous _____ showing?	Est-ce un spectacle permanent? *ehs uhn spehktahkl pehrmahnohn?*

What's on at...? _____	Qu'y a-t-il au...?
	kee yah teel oa...?
– the theatre? _____	Qu'y a-t-il au théâtre?
	kee yah teel oa tayahtr?
– the concert hall? _____	Qu'y a-t-il à la salle des concerts?
	kee yah teel ah lah sahl day kawnsehr?
– the opera? _____	Qu'y a-t-il à l'opéra?
	kee yah teel ah loapayrah?
Where can I find a _____ gooddisco around here?	Où se trouve une bonne disco par ici?
	oo suh troov ewn bon deeskoa pahr eesee?
Is it members only? ____	Exige-t-on une carte de membre?
	ehgzeejh-tawn ewn kahrt duh mohnbr?
Where can I find a _____ good nightclub around here?	Où se trouve une bonne boîte de nuit par ici?
	oo suh troov ewn bon bwaht duh nwee pahr eesee?
Is it evening wear_____ only?	La tenue de soirée, est-elle obligatoire?
	lah tuhnew duh swahray, eh tehl obleegahtwahr?
Should I/we dress up? _	La tenue de soirée, est-elle souhaitée?
	lah tuhnew duh swahray ehtehl sooehtay?
What time does the _____ show start?	A quelle heure commence la représentation?
	ah kehl uhr komohns lah ruhprayzohntahsyawn?
When's the next _____ soccer match?	Quand est le prochain match de football?
	kohn teh luh proshahn mahtch duh footbohl?
Who's playing? _____	Qui joue contre qui?
	kee jhoo kawntr kee?
I'd like an escort for_____ tonight. Could you arrange that for me?	Je veux une hôtesse pour ce soir. Pouvez-vous arranger ça?
	jhuh vuh zewn oatehs poor suh swahr. poovay voo zahrohnjhay sah?

11.3 Booking tickets

Could you book some tickets for us?	Pouvez-vous nous faire une réservation?
	poovay voo noo fehr ewn rayzehrvahsyawn?
We'd like to book... seats/a table...	Nous voulons...places/une table...
	noo voolawn...plahs/ewn tahbl...
– in the stalls	Nous voulons...places à l'orchestre.
	noo voolawn...plahs ah lorkehstr
– on the balcony	Nous voulons...places au balcon.
	noo voolawn...plahs oa bahlkawn
– box seats	Nous voulons...places dans les loges.
	noo voolawn...plahs dohn lay lojh
– a table at the front	Nous voulons...une table à l'avant.
	noo voolawn...ewn tahbl ah lahvohn
– in the middle	Nous voulons...places au milieu.
	noo voolawn...plahs oa meelyuh
– at the back	Nous voulons...places à l'arrière.
	noo voolawn...plahs ah lahryehr
Could I book... seats for the...o'clock performance?	Puis-je réserver...places pour la représentation de...heures?
	pwee jhuh rayzehrvay...plahs poor lah ruhprayzohntahsyawn duh...uhr?
Are there any seats left for tonight?	Reste-t-il encore des places pour ce soir?
	rehst-uh-teel ohnkor day plahs poor suh swahr?
How much is a ticket?	Combien coûte un billet?
	kawnbyahn koot uhn beeyeh?
When can I pick the tickets up?	Quand puis-je venir chercher les billets?
	kohn pwee jhuh vuhneer shehrshay lay beeyeh?
I've got a reservation	J'ai réservé
	jhay rayzehrvay
My name's...	Mon nom est...
	mawn nawn eh...

Vous voulez réserver pour quelle représentation?	Which performance do you want to book for?
Où voulez-vous vous asseoir?	Where would you like to sit?
Tout est vendu	Everything's sold out
Il ne reste que des places debout	We've only got standing spaces left
Il ne reste que des places au balcon	We've only got balcony seats left
Il ne reste que des places au poulailler	We've only got seats left in the gallery
Il ne reste que des places d'orchestre	We've only got stalls seats left
Il ne reste que des places à l'avant	We've only got seats left at the front
Il ne reste que des places à l'arrière	We've only got seats left at the back
Combien de places voulez-vous?	How many seats would you like?
Vous devez venir chercher les billets avant...heures	You'll have to pick up the tickets before...o'clock
Puis-je voir vos billets?	Tickets, please
Voici votre place	This is your seat
Vous n'êtes pas aux bonnes places	You're in the wrong seats

12
Sports

12.1 Sporting questions

Where can we... around here?	Où pouvons-nous...?
	oo poovawn noo...?
Is there a... around here?	Y a-t-il un...dans les environs?
	ee yah teel uhn...dohn lay zohnveerawn?
Can I hire a...here?	Puis-je louer un...ici?
	pwee jhuh looay uhn...eesee?
Can I take...lessons?	Puis-je prendre des cours de...?
	pwee jhuh prohndr day koor duh...?
How much is that per hour/per day/a turn?	Quel est le prix à l'heure/à la journée/à chaque fois?
	kehl eh luh pree ah luhr/ah lah jhoornay/ah shahk fwah?
Do I need a permit for that?	A-t-on besoin d'un permis?
	ah tawn buhzwawn duhn pehrmee?
Where can I get the permit?	Où puis-je obtenir le permis?
	oo pwee jhuh obtuhneer luh pehrmee?

12.2 By the waterfront

Is it a long way to the sea still?	La mer, est-elle encore loin?
	lah mehr eh tehl ohnkor lwahn?
Is there a...around here?	Y a-t-il un...dans les environs?
	ee yah teel uhn...dohn lay zohnveerawn?
– a public swimming pool	Y a-t-il une piscine dans les environs?
	ee yah teel ewn peeseen dohn lay zohnveerawn?
– a sandy beach	Y a-t-il une plage de sable dans les environs?
	ee yah teel ewn plahjh duh sahbl dohn lay zohnveerawn?

– a nudist beach_____	Y a-t-il une plage pour nudistes dans les environs?
	ee yah teel ewn plahjh poor newdeest dohn lay zohnveerawn?
– mooring _____	Y a-t-il un embarcadère pour les bateaux dans les environs?
	ee yah teel uhn nohnbahrkahdehr poor lay bahtoa dohn lay zohnveerawn?
Are there any rocks ____ here?	Y a-t-il aussi des rochers ici?
	ee yah teel oasee day roshay eesee?
When's high/low tide?__	Quand est la marée haute/basse?
	kohn teh lah mahray oat/bahs?
What's the water _____ temperature?	Quelle est la température de l'eau?
	kehl eh lah tohnpayratewr duh loa?
Is it (very) deep here? __	Est-ce (très) profond ici?
	ehs (treh) proafawn eesee?
Can you stand here? ___	A-t-on pied ici?
	ah tawn pyay eesee?
Is it safe to swim here?_	Peut-on nager en sécurité ici?
	puh tawn nahjhay ohn saykewreetay eesee?
Are there any currents?_	Y a-t-il des courants?
	ee yah teel day koorohn?
Are there any rapids/___ waterfalls in this river?	Est-ce que cette rivière a des courants rapides/des chutes d'eau?
	ehs kuh seht reevyehr ah day koorohn rahpeed/day shewt doa?
What does that flag/ ___ buoy mean?	Que signifie ce drapeau/cette bouée là-bas?
	kuh seenyeefee suh drahpoa/seht booway lah bah?

Danger	Pêche interdite	Baignade interdite
Danger	No fishing	No swimming
Pêche	Surf interdit	Seulement avec
Fishing water	No surfing	permis Permits only

Is there a life guard on duty here?	Y a-t-il un maître nageur qui surveille?
	ee yah teel uhn mehtr nahjhuhr kee sewrvehy?
Are dogs allowed here?	Les chiens sont admis ici?
	lay shyahn sawn tahdmee eesee?
Is camping on the beach allowed?	Peut-on camper sur la plage?
	puh tawn kohnpay sewr lah plahjh?
Are we allowed to build a fire here?	Peut-on faire un feu ici?
	puh tawn fehr uhn fuh eesee?

12.3 In the snow

Can I take ski lessons here?	Puis-je prendre des leçons de ski?
	pwee jhuh prohndr day luhsawn duh skee?
for beginners/ advanced	pour débutants/initiés
	poor daybewtohn/eeneesyay
How large are the groups?	Quelle est la taille des groupes?
	kehl eh lah tahy day groop?
What language are the classes in?	En quelle langue donne-t-on les leçons de ski?
	ohn kehl lohng don tawn lay luhsawn duh skee?
I'd like a lift pass, please	Je voudrais un abonnement pour les remontées mécaniques.
	jhuh voodreh zuhn nahbonmohn poor lay ruhmawntay maykahneek
Must I give you a passport photo?	Dois-je donner une photo d'identité?
	dwah jhuh donay ewn foatoa deedohnteetay?
Where can I have a passport photo taken?	Où puis-je faire faire une photo d'identité?
	oo pwee jhuh fehr fehr ewn foatoa deedohnteetay?

Where are the _____ beginners' slopes?	Où sont les pistes de ski pour débutants?
	oo sawn lay peest duh skee poor daybewtohn?
Are there any runs for __ cross-country skiing?	Y a-t-il des pistes de ski de fond dans les environs?
	ee yah teel day peest duh skee duh fawn dohn lay zohnveerawn?
Have the cross- _____ country runs been marked?	Les pistes de ski de fond, sont-elles indiquées?
	lay peest duh skee duh fawn, sawn tehl ahndeekay?
Are the...in operation? __	Est-ce que les...marchent?
	ehs kuh lay...mahrsh?
– the ski lifts _____	Est-ce que les remontées mécaniques marchent?
	ehs kuh lay ruhmawntay maykahneek mahrsh?
– the chair lifts _____	Est-ce que les télésièges marchent?
	ehs kuh lay taylaysyehjh mahrsh?
Are the slopes usable? _	Est-ce que les pistes sont ouvertes?
	ehs kuh lay peest sawn toovehrt?
Are the cross-country __ runs usable?	Est-ce que les pistes de ski de fond sont ouvertes?
	ehs kuh lay peest duh skee duh fawn sawn toovehrt?

13

Sickness

13.1 Call (fetch) the doctor

Could you call/fetch a __ doctor quickly, please?	Voulez-vous vite appeler/aller chercher un médecin s'il vous plaît?
	voolay voo veet ahpuhlay/ahlay shehrshay uhn maydsahn seel voo pleh?
When does the doctor _ have surgery?	Quand est-ce que le médecin reçoit?
	kohn tehs kuh luh maydsahn ruhswah?
When can the doctor___ come?	Quand est-ce que le médecin peut venir?
	kohn tehs kuh luh maydsahn puh vuhneer?
I'd like to make an _____ appointment to see the doctor	Pouvez-vous me prendre un rendez-vous chez le médecin?
	poovay voo muh prohndr uhn rohnday voo shay luh maydsahn?
I've got an _____ appointment to see the doctor at...	J'ai un rendez-vous chez le médecin à...heures
	jhay uhn rohnday voo shay luh maydsahn a...uhr
Which doctor/chemist __ has night/weekend duty?	Quel médecin/Quelle pharmacie est de garde cette nuit/ce week-end?
	kehl maydsahn/kehl fahrmahsee eh duh gahrd seht nwee/suh week-ehnd?

13.2 Patient's ailments

I don't feel well _____	Je ne me sens pas bien
	jhuh nuh muh sohn pah byahn
I'm dizzy_____	J'ai des vertiges
	jhay day vehrteejh
– ill_____	Je suis malade
	jhuh swee mahlahd
– sick _____	J'ai mal au coeur
	jhay mahl oa kuhr

I've got a cold_____	Je suis enrhumé(e)
	jhuh swee zohnrewmay
It hurts here_____	J'ai mal ici
	jhay mahl eesee
I've been throwing up __	J'ai vomi
	jhay vomee
I've got... _____	Je souffre de...
	jhuh soofr duh...
I'm running a_____ temperature	J'ai de la fièvre
	jhayduh lah fyehvr
I've been stung by _____ a wasp.	J'ai été piqué(e) par une guêpe
	jhay aytay peekay pahr ewn gehp
I've been stung by an __ insect	J'ai été piqué(e) par un insecte
	jhay aytay peekay pahr uhn nahnsehkt
I've been bitten by_____ a dog	J'ai été mordu(e) par un chien
	jhay aytay mordew pahr uhn shyahn
I've been stung by _____ a jellyfish	J'ai été piqué(e) par une méduse
	jhay aytay peekay pahr ewn maydewz
I've been bitten by_____ a snake	J'ai été mordu(e) par un serpent
	jhay aytay mordew pahr uhn sehrpohn
I've been bitten by_____ an animal	J'ai été mordu(e) par un animal
	jhay aytay mordew pahr uhn nahneemahl
I've cut myself _____	Je me suis coupé(e)
	jhuh muh swee koopay
I've burned myself _____	Je me suis brûlé(e)
	jhuh muh swee brewlay
I've grazed myself _____	Je me suis égratigné(e)
	jhuh muh swee zaygrahteenyay
I've had a fall _____	Je suis tombé(e)
	jhuh swee tawnbay
I've sprained my ankle _	Je me suis foulé(e) la cheville
	jhuh muh swee foolay lah shuhveey
I've come for the _____ morning-after pill	Je viens pour la pilule du lendemain
	jhuh vyahn poor lah peelewl dew lohndmahn

13.3 The consultation

Quels sont vos symptômes?	What seems to be the problem?
Depuis combien de temps avez-vous ces symptômes?	How long have you had these symptoms?
Avez-vous eu ces symptômes auparavant?	Have you had this trouble before?
Avez-vous de la fièvre?	How high is your temperature?
Déshabillez-vous s'il vous plaît?	Get undressed, please
Pouvez-vous vous mettre torse nu?	Strip to the waist, please
Vous pouvez vous déshabiller là-bas.	You can undress there
Pouvez-vous remonter la manche de votre bras gauche/droit?	Roll up your left/right sleeve, please
Allongez-vous ici	Lie down here, please
Ceci vous fait mal?	Does this hurt?
Aspirez et expirez profondément	Breathe deeply
Ouvrez la bouche	Open your mouth

Patient's medical history

I'm a diabetic_____ Je suis diabétique
jhuh swee dyahbayteek

I have a heart _____ Je suis cardiaque
condition *jhuh swee kahrdyahk*

I have asthma _____ J'ai de l'asthme
jhay duh lahsm

I'm allergic to..._____ Je suis allergique à...
jhuh swee zahlehrjheek ah...

I'm...months pregnant	Je suis enceinte de...mois
	jhuh swee zohnsahnt duh...mwah
I'm on a diet	Je suis au régime
	jhuh swee zoa rayjheem
I'm on medication/the pill	Je prends des médicaments/la pilule
	jhuh prohn day maydeekahmohn/lah peelewl
I've had a heart attack once before	J'ai déjà eu une crise cardiaque
	jhay dayjhah ew ewn kreez kahrdyahk
I've had a(n)...operation	J'ai été opéré(e) de...
	jhay aytay oapayray duh...
I've been ill recently	Je viens d'être malade
	jhuh vyahn dehtr mahlahd
I've got an ulcer	J'ai un ulcère à l'estomac
	jhay uhn newlsehr ah lehstomah
I've got my period	J'ai mes règles
	jhay may rehgl

Avez-vous des allergies?	Do you have any allergies?
Prenez-vous des médicaments?	Are you on any medication?
Suivez-vous un régime?	Are you on any sort of diet?
Etes-vous enceinte?	Are you pregnant?
Etes-vous vacciné(e) contre le tétanos?	Have you had a tetanus vaccination?

The diagnosis

Is it contagious?	Est-ce contagieux?
	ehs kawntahjhyuh?
How long do I have to stay...?	Combien de temps dois-je rester...?
	kawnbyahn duh tohn dwah jhuh rehstay...?
– in bed	Combien de temps dois-je rester au lit?
	kawnbyahn duh tohn dwah jhuh rehstay oa lee?

Ce n'est rien de grave	It's nothing serious
Vous vous êtes cassé le/la...	Your...is broken
Vous vous êtes foulé le/la...	You've sprained your...
Vous vous êtes déchiré le/la...	You've got a torn...
Vous avez une inflammation	You've got an inflammation
Vous avez une crise d'appendicite	You've got appendicitis
Vous avez une bronchite	You've got bronchitis
Vous avez une maladie vénérienne	You've got a venereal disease
Vous avez une grippe	You've got the flu
Vous avez eu une crise cardiaque	You've had a heart attack
Vous avez une infection (virale/bactérielle)	You've got an infection (viral/bacterial)
Vous avez une pneumonie	You've got pneumonia
Vous avez un ulcère à l'estomac	You've got an ulcer
Vous vous êtes froissé un muscle	You've pulled a muscle

– in hospital_____	Combien de temps dois-je rester à l'hôpital?
	kawnbyahn duh tohn dwah jhuh rehstay ah loapeetahl?
Do I have to go on ____ a special diet?	Dois-je suivre un régime?
	dwah jhuh sweevr uhn rayjheem?
Am I allowed to travel? _	Puis-je voyager?
	pwee jhuh vwahyahjhay?
Can I make a new ____ appointment?	Puis-je prendre un autre rendez-vous?
	pwee jhuh prohndr uhn noatr rohnday voo?

Vous avez une infection vaginale	You've got a vaginal infection
Vous avez une intoxication alimentaire	You've got food poisoning
Vous avez une insolation	You've got sunstroke
Vous êtes allergique à...	You're allergic to...
Vous êtes enceinte	You're pregnant
Je veux faire analyser votre sang/urine/vos selles	I'd like to have your blood/urine/stools tested
Il faut faire des points de suture	It needs stitching
Je vous envoie à un spécialiste/l'hôpital	I'm referring you to a specialist/sending you to hospital.
Il faut faire des radios	You'll need to have some x-rays taken
Voulez-vous reprendre place un petitinstant dans la salle d'attente?	Could you wait in the waiting room, please?
Il faut vous opérer	You'll need an operation

When do I have to _____ come back?	Quand dois-je revenir?	*kohn dwah jhuh ruhvuhneer?*
I'll come back _____ tomorrow	Je reviendrai demain	*jhuh ruhvyahndray duhmahn*

Vous devez revenir demain/dans...jours	Come back tomorrow/in...days' time

13.4 Medication and prescriptions

How do I take this _____ medicine? — Comment dois-je prendre ces médicaments?
komohn dwah jhuh prohndr say maydeekahmohn?

How many capsules/___ drops/injections/ spoonfuls/ tablets each time? — Combien de capsules/gouttes/piqûres/ cuillères/comprimés à chaque fois?
kawnbyahn duh kahpsewl/goot/peekewr/ kweeyehr/kawnpreemay ah shahk fwah?

How many times a _____ day? — Combien de fois par jour?
kawnbyahn duh fwah pahr jhoor?

I've forgotten my _____ medication. At home I take... — J'ai oublié mes médicaments. A la maison je prends...
jhay oobleeyay may maydeekahmohn. ah lah mehzawn jhuh prohn...

Could you make out a___ prescription for me? — Pouvez-vous me faire une ordonnance?
poovay voo muh fehr ewn ordonohns?

---

avaler entièrement swallow whole	cuillerées (...à soupe/...à café) spoonfuls (tablespoons/ teaspoons)	pendant...jours for...days
avant chaque repas before meals		piqûres injections
capsules capsules	dissoudre dans l'eau dissolve in water	pommade ointment
la prise de ce médicament peut rendre dangereuse la conduite automobile this medication impairs your driving	enduire rub on	prendre take
	finir le traitement finish the course	toutes les...heures every...hours
	...fois par jour ...times a day	uniquement pour usage externe not for internal use
comprimés tablets	gouttes drops	

Je vous prescris un antibiotique/un sirop/un tranquillisant/un calmant	I'm prescribing antibiotics/a mixture/a tranquillizer/pain killer
Vous devez rester au calme	Have lots of rest
Vous ne devez pas sortir	Stay indoors
Vous devez rester au lit	Stay in bed

13.5 At the dentist's

Do you know a good ___ dentist?	Connaissez-vous un bon dentiste?
	konehsay voo zuhn bawn dohnteest?
Could you make a ___ dentist's appointment for me? It's urgent	Pouvez-vous me prendre un rendez-vous chez le dentiste? C'est urgent
	poovay voo muh prohndr uhn rohnday voo shay luh dohnteest? seh tewrjhohn
Can I come in today, ___ please?	Puis-je venir aujourd'hui s'il vous plaît?
	pwee jhuh vuhneer oajhoordwee seel voo pleh?
I have (terrible) ___ toothache	J'ai une rage de dents/un mal de dents (épouvantable)
	jhay ewn rahjh duh dohn/uhn mahl duh dohn (aypoovohntahbl)
Could you prescribe/___ give me a painkiller?	Pouvez-vous me prescrire/donner un calmant?
	poovay voo muh prehskreer/donay uhn kahlmohn?
A piece of my tooth ___ has broken off	Ma dent s'est cassée
	mah dohn seh kahssay
My filling's come out ___	Mon plombage est parti
	mawn plawnbahjh eh pahrtee
I've got a broken ___ crown	Ma couronne est cassée
	mah kooron eh kahssay

I'd like/I don't want a___ local anaesthetic	Je (ne) veux (pas) une anesthésie locale *jhuh (nuh) vuh (paz) ewn ahnehstayzee lokahl*
Can you do a _____ makeshift repair job?	Pouvez-vous me soigner de façon provisoire? *poovay voo muh swahnyay duh fahsawn proveezwahr?*
I don't want this tooth___ pulled	Je ne veux pas que cette dent soit arrachée *jhuh nuh vuh pah kuh seht dohn swaht ahrahshay*
My dentures are _____ broken. Can you fix them?	Mon dentier est cassé. Pouvez-vous le réparer? *mawn dohntyay eh kahssay. poovay voo luh raypahray?*

☞

Quelle dent/molaire vous fait mal?	Which tooth hurts?
Vous avez un abcès	You've got an abscess
Je dois faire une dévitalisation	I'll have to do a root canal
Je vais vous faire une anesthésie locale	I'm giving you a local anaesthetic
Je dois plomber/extraire/polir cette dent	I'll have to fill/pull/file this tooth
Je dois utiliser la roulette	I'll have to drill
Ouvrez bien la bouche	Open your mouth
Fermez la bouche	Close your mouth
Rincez	Rinse
Sentez-vous encore la douleur?	Does it hurt still?

14

In trouble

14.1 Asking for help

Help! _____	Au secours! *oa suhkoor!*
Fire! _____	Au feu! *oa fuh!*
Police! _____	Police! *pohlees!*
Quick! _____	Vite! *veet!*
Danger! _____	Danger! *dohnjhay*
Watch out! _____	Attention! *ahtohnsyawn!*
Stop! _____	Stop! *stop!*
Be careful! _____	Prudence! *prewdohns!*
Don't! _____	Arrêtez! *ahrehtay!*
Let go! _____	Lâchez! *lahshay!*
Stop that thief! _____	Au voleur! *oa voluhr!*
Could you help me, ____ please?	Voulez-vous m'aider? *voolay voo mayday?*
Where's the police ____ station/emergency exit/fire escape?	Où est le poste de police/la sortie de secours/l'escalier de secours? *oo eh luh post duh polees/lah sortee duh suhkoor/lehskahlyay duh suhkoor?*
Where's the nearest ____ fire extinguisher?	Où y a-t-il un extincteur? *oo ee yah teel uhn nehxtahnktuhr?*
Call the fire brigade! ____	Prévenez les sapeurs-pompiers! *prayvuhnay lay sahpuhr pawnpyay!*
Call the police! _____	Appelez la police! *ahpuhlay lah polees!*
Call an ambulance! ____	Appelez une ambulance! *ahpuhlay ewn ohnbewlohns!*
Where's the nearest ____ phone?	Où est le téléphone le plus proche? *oo eh luh taylayfon luh plew prosh?*
Could I use your ____ phone?	Puis-je utiliser votre téléphone? *pwee jhuh ewteeleezay votr taylayfon?*
What's the emergency _ number?	Quel est le numéro d'urgence? *kehl eh luh newmayroa dewrjhohns?*
What's the number for _ the police?	Quel est le numéro de téléphone de la police? *kehl eh luh newmayroa duh taylayfon duh lah polees?*

14.2 Loss

I've lost my purse/ _____ wallet	J'ai perdu mon porte-monnaie/ portefeuille
	jhay pehrdew mawn port moneh/portfuhy
I lost my...yesterday _____	Hier j'ai oublié mon/ma...
	yehr jhay oobleeay mawn/mah...
I left my...here _____	J'ai laissé mon/ma...ici
	jhay layssay mawn/mah...eesee
Did you find my...? _____	Avez-vous trouvé mon/ma...?
	ahvay voo troovay mawn/mah...?
It was right here _____	Il était là
	eel ayteh lah
It's quite valuable _____	C'est un objet de valeur
	seh tuhn nobjheh duh vahluhr
Where's the lost _____ property office?	Où est le bureau des objets trouvés?
	oo eh luh bewroa day zobjheh troovay?

14.3 Accidents

There's been an _____ accident	Il y a eu un accident
	eel ee yah ew uhn nahkseedohn
Someone's fallen into __ the water	Quelqu'un est tombé dans l'eau
	kehlkuhn eh tawnbay dohn loa
There's a fire _____	Il y a un incendie.
	eel ee yah uhn nahnsohndee
Is anyone hurt? _____	Y a-t-il quelqu'un de blessé?
	ee yah teel kehlkuhn duh blehssay?
Some people have _____ been/no one's been injured	Il (n)y a des(pas de) blessés
	eel (n)ee yah day(pah duh) blehssay
There's someone in _____ the car/train still	Il y a encore quelqu'un dans la voiture/le train
	eel ee ah ohnkor kehlkuhn dohn lah vwahtewr/luh trahn

It's not too bad. Don't __ worry	Ce n'est pas si grave. Ne vous inquiétez pas
	suh neh pah see grahv. nuh voo zahnkyaytay pah
Leave everything the __ way it is, please	Ne touchez à rien s'il vous plaît
	nuh tooshay ah ryahn seel voo pleh
I want to talk to the ____ police first	Je veux d'abord parler à la police
	jhuh vuh dahbor pahrlay ah lah polees
I want to take a_____ photo first	Je veux d'abord prendre une photo
	jhuh vuh dahbor prohndr ewn foatoa
Here's my name _____ and address	Voici mon nom et mon adresse
	vwahsee mawn nawn ay mawn nahdrehs
Could I have your_____ name and address?	Puis-je connaître votre nom et votre adresse?
	pwee jhuh konehtr votr nawn ay votr ahdrehs?
Could I see some_____ identification/your insurance papers?	Puis-je voir vos papiers d'identité/papiers d'assurance?
	pwee jhuh vwahr voa pahpyay deedohnteetay/pahpyay dahsewrohns?
Will you act as a_____ witness?	Voulez-vous être témoin?
	voolay voo zehtr taymwahn?
I need the details for __ the insurance	Je dois avoir les données pour l'assurance.
	jhuh dwah zahvwahr lay donay poor lahsewrohns
Are you insured? _____	Etes-vous assuré? *eht voo zahsewray?*
Third party or _____ comprehensive?	Responsabilité civile ou tous risques?
	rehspawnsahbeeleetay seeveel oo too reesk?
Could you sign here, ___ please?	Voulez-vous signer ici?
	voolay voo seenyay eesee?

14.4 Theft

I've been robbed _____	On m'a volé. *awn mah volay*
My...has been stolen ___	Mon/ma...a été volé(e). *mawn/mah...ah aytay volay*
My car's been _____ broken into	On a cambriolé ma voiture. *awn nah kohnbreeolay mah vwahtewr*

14.5 Missing person

I've lost my child/_____ grandmother	J'ai perdu mon enfant/ma grand-mère *jhay pehrdew mawn nohnfohn/mah grohnmehr*
Could you help me _____ find him/her?	Voulez-vous m'aider à le/la chercher? *voolay voo mayday ah luh/lah shehrshay?*
Have you seen a _____ small child?	Avez-vous vu un petit enfant? *ahvay voo vew uhn puhtee tohnfohn?*
He's/she's...years old __	Il/elle a...ans. *eel/ehl ah...ohn*
He's/she's got_____ short/long/blond/red/ brown/black/grey/ curly/ straight/frizzy hair	Il/elle a les cheveux courts/longs/blonds/ roux/bruns/noirs/gris/bouclés/raides/ frisés *eel/ehl ah lay shuhvuh koor/lawn/blawn/roo/bruhn/nwahr/gree rehd/freezay*
with a ponytail _____	avec une queue de cheval *ahvehk ewn kuh duh shuhvahl*
with plaits _____	avec des nattes *ahvehk day naht*
in a bun _____	avec un chignon *ahvehk uhn sheenyawn*
He's/she's got_____ blue/brown/green eyes	Il/elle a les yeux bleus/bruns/verts *eel/ehl ah lay zyuh bluh/bruhn/vehr*

He's wearing _____ swimming trunks/ mountaineering boots	Il porte un maillot de bain/des chaussures de montagne. *eel port uhn mahyoa duh bahn/day shoasewr duh mawntahnyuh*
with/without glasses/ __ a bag	avec/sans lunettes/un sac *ahvehk/sohn lewneht/uhn sahk*
tall/short_____	grand(e)/petit(e) *grohn(d)/puhtee(t)*
This is a photo of_____ him/her	Voici une photo de lui/d'elle. *vwahsee ewn foatoa duh lwee/dehl*
He/she must be lost ___	Il/elle s'est certainement égaré(e). *eel/ehl seh sehrtehnmohn aygahray*

14.6 The police

An arrest

Vos papiers de voiture s'il vous plaît.	Your registration papers, please
Vous rouliez trop vite	You were speeding
Vous êtes en stationnement interdit	You're not allowed to park here
Vous n'avez pas mis d'argent dans le parcmètre	You haven't put money in the meter
Vos phares ne marchent pas	Your lights aren't working
Vous avez une contravention de...euros	That's a...euro fine
Vous voulez payer immédiatement?	Do you want to pay on the spot?
Vous devez payer immédiatement	You'll have to pay on the spot

I don't speak French ___	Je ne parle pas français. *jhuh nuh pahrl pah frohnseh*

I didn't see the sign ____	Je n'ai pas vu ce panneau.
	jhuh nay pah vew suh pahnoa
I don't understand ____ what it says	Je ne comprends pas ce qu'il y est écrit.
	jhuh nuh kawnprohn pah suh keel ee yeh taykree
I was only doing... ____ kilometres an hour	Je ne roulais qu'à...kilomètres à l'heure.
	jhuh nuh rooleh kah...keeloamehtr ah luhr
I'll have my car ____ checked	Je vais faire réviser ma voiture.
	jhuh veh fehr rayveezay mah vwahtewr
I was blinded by ____ oncoming lights	J'ai été aveuglé(e) par une voiture en sens inverse.
	jhay aytay ahvuhglay pahr ewn vwahtewr ohn sohns ahnvehrs

At the police station

Où est-ce arrivé?	Where did it happen?
Qu'avez-vous perdu?	What's missing?
Qu'a-t-on volé?	What's been taken?
Puis-je voir vos papiers d'identité?	Do you have some identification?
A quelle heure est-ce arrivé?	What time did it happen?
Qui est en cause?	Who are the others?
Y a-t-il des témoins?	Are there any witnesses?
Voulez-vous remplir ceci?	Fill this out, please
Signez ici s'il vous plaît	Sign here, please
Voulez-vous un interprète?	Do you want an interpreter?

I want to report a ____ collision/missing person/rape	Je viens faire la déclaration d'une collision/d'une disparition/d'un viol
	jhuh vyahn fehr lah dayklahrasyawn dewn koleezyawn/dewn deespahreesyawn/duhn vyol

Could you make out ___ a report, please?	Voulez-vous faire un rapport? *voolay voo fehr uhn rahpor?*
Could I have a copy ___ for the insurance?	Puis-je avoir une copie pour l'assurance? *pwee jhahvwahr ewn kopee poor lahsewrohns?*
I've lost everything_____	J'ai tout perdu *jhay too pehrdew*
I'd like an interpreter ___	J'aimerais un interprète *jhehmuhreh zuhn nahntehrpreht*
I'm innocent _____	Je suis innocent(e) *jhuh swee zeenosohn(t)*
I don't know anything __ about it	Je ne sais rien *jhuh nuh seh ryahn*
I want to speak to _____ someone from the British consulate	Je veux parler à quelqu'un du consulat britannique *jhuh vuh pahrlay ah kehlkuhn dew kawnsewlah breetahneek*
I need to see someone _ from the British embassy	Je dois parler à quelqu'un de l'ambassade britannique *jhuh dwah pahrlay ah kehlkuhn duh lohnbahsahd breetahneek*
I want a lawyer who_____ speaks English	Je veux un avocat qui parle anglais *jhuh vuh uhn nahvokah kee pahrl ohngleh*